When it's raining, umbrellas and shoes often come to our rescue. Shoes come in handy when there are puddles everywhere. Have you ever wondered what the first umbrella looked like? Or how long shoes have been around? You can find out on pages 22 and 4.

There are many ordinary things in the bathroom—from your toothbrush and toothpaste to the mirror, sink, and bathtub. But the story of their origin isn't ordinary at all. Do you want to know more? Turn to page 68!

ENCYCLOPEDIA
OF ORDINARY
THINGS

Written by Štěpánka Sekaninová

Illustrations by Eva Chupíková

Albatros

TABLE OF CONTENTS

SHOES

Have you ever had the most splintery splinter stuck in your foot? Ouch! If you have, then you know it hurts like heck. Just take a stroll around the garden as you are—with bare feet. Picture it: dewy grass, the rising sun. You want to enjoy nature with all your senses but uh-oh! Your pampered feet immediately start protesting: "Help! What are you doing to us, you silly little human? The pebbles are sharp, the twigs prickly, and the grass tickles. Put on your shoes, right now! Phew, what a relief. Hail to the genius who invented shoes." Well yeah, but who was it? And what's the story of shoes, anyway?

PREHISTORY

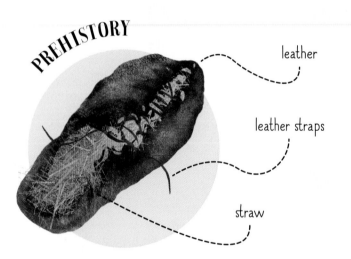

leather

leather straps

straw

Why bears, exactly?

The soles of some prehistoric shoes were made from bear skin. But why bear skin? It's thinner than cowhide and it's not waterproof. The answer is simple. Our ancestors believed that bear skin would give them the strength of this feared animal and protect them.

The first shoemakers

Which material was used to make shoes in prehistoric times? That's a no-brainer! Plant fiber, bamboo, or palm leaves were more than enough to sew a pair of sandals. If you wanted sturdier footwear, you needed leather or fur.

The Ice Age is coming

Even our prehistoric ancestors used to wear shoes. That's because back then, they traveled from warm Africa all the way up north. Unaccustomed to the cold, they immediately went about inventing clothing which would allow them to survive local winters. And since freezing weather didn't do any good to one's feet either, they came up with the first shoes to wear with their coats. The **first "shoes"** ever found were made in the Stone Age and boast an impressive 7,800 years of age.

TIMELINE ⟶

| PREHISTORY | ANCIENT EGYPT | ANCIENT GREECE | ANCIENT ROME |

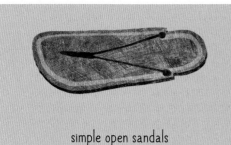

simple open sandals

sandals with toe protection

later sandals
with heel protection

Keep an eye on my shoes

Prehistoric times were followed by antiquity—and by masters of the shoemaking craft as well. These men could weave **sandals from tiny strips**, but also sew hard low-top shoes or rainproof high boots. In Egypt, the job was pretty easy since the hot arid climate required simple shoes—leather sandals that looked like the flip-flops we love today. They were worn mostly by rich men, and also the Pharaoh. When the Pharaoh grew tired of wearing shoes, he entrusted them to one of his servants, a so-called sandal-bearer.

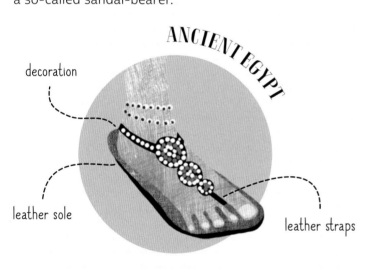

ANCIENT EGYPT

decoration

leather sole

leather straps

The Pharaoh's shoes were decorated with beads, gold, semi-precious stones (e.g., carnelian), and precious stones (lapis lazuli, etc.).

Shoe production in Egypt

The leather that went into Egyptian sandals was soft and supple. That's because shoemakers would soak them in a **special oily liquid**. This would allow the wearers to march through large puddles—if there were any puddles in Ancient Egypt, that is—without having to worry about water soaking through, or about the footwear slowly but surely rotting away.

THE MIDDLE AGES   THE RENAISSANCE   THE BAROQUE   19TH CENTURY

Diverse antiquity

While only men could enjoy footwear in Egypt, with their significant others stumbling around barefoot, Greek women pampered their feet in **Persikai** shoes, sown from the softest light leather. If you wanted to take the strain off your feet, you went for **Syconias** (a)—strap sandals. Tougher gentlemen wore **Karbantines** (b)—a strip of leather wrapped around the foot and tied with strings on the instep.

Greek woman with Persikai shoes.

ANCIENT GREECE

Karbatine shoes were made from a single piece of leather.

Syconia, a type of Greek shoe, consisted of interlaced straps.

These shoes later inspired Roman shoemakers.

Persikais—typical female footwear

a   b

Caliage shoes

ANCIENT ROME

Their lacing reached high above the ankle.

Roman nobleman with Calcei shoes.

Vain Romans

Save your sandals for home, thought Romans while strolling in the streets, wearing lace-up shoes which reached up to their mid-calves—so-called **Calceis**. The rich and noble preferred them to be made in an attractive **red color**, while the serious-minded senators opted for the **elegant black**. Meanwhile, tough Roman soldiers wouldn't wear anything if its soles weren't reinforced with nails—to keep sleepiness at bay.

Calcei shoes—strap sandals
a—These high-top leather shoes were tied around the wearer's calves with straps.
b—Red Calceis were worn by Roman nobles, while commoners had black ones.
c—Detail of the sole of a military shoe fitted with nails.

c

THE MIDDLE AGES   THE RENAISSANCE

THE BAROQUE   19TH CENTURY

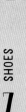

SHOES

7

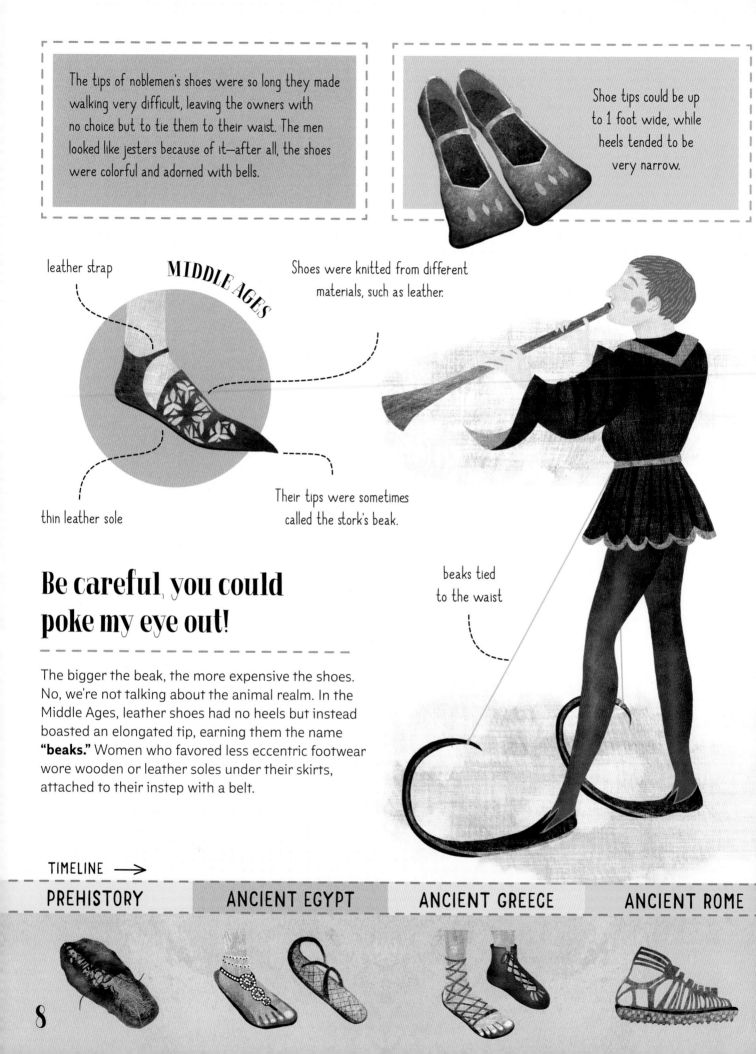

The tips of noblemen's shoes were so long they made walking very difficult, leaving the owners with no choice but to tie them to their waist. The men looked like jesters because of it—after all, the shoes were colorful and adorned with bells.

Shoe tips could be up to 1 foot wide, while heels tended to be very narrow.

leather strap

MIDDLE AGES

Shoes were knitted from different materials, such as leather.

thin leather sole

Their tips were sometimes called the stork's beak.

Be careful, you could poke my eye out!

The bigger the beak, the more expensive the shoes. No, we're not talking about the animal realm. In the Middle Ages, leather shoes had no heels but instead boasted an elongated tip, earning them the name **"beaks."** Women who favored less eccentric footwear wore wooden or leather soles under their skirts, attached to their instep with a belt.

beaks tied to the waist

TIMELINE $\longrightarrow$

| PREHISTORY | ANCIENT EGYPT | ANCIENT GREECE | ANCIENT ROME |

8

These extravagant shoes remained fashionable for 100 years.

Complicated embroidery was sometimes underlined by golden ornaments.

THE RENAISSANCE

The soles were made from cork or wood.

Shoes were tied with a silk ribbon.

Just don't swallow me, OK?

While the Middle Ages elongated, the Renaissance broadened. What do we mean? Shoe tips. Long beaks were replaced with **duckbills** or **cow mouths**—wide tips that needed to be padded in order for the shoes to be worn. What colors were fashionable back then? Yellow, red, blue, pink, black, and green. Materials? Soft leather and luxury textiles. Which shape was in fashion? Low flat shoes the wearer had to tie to their feet. Ladies, however, would ruin their feet in ultrahigh platform heels of 1.6 feet—nothing to sneer at. No wonder the stumbling fops had to be physically supported.

Shoes like these were worn long ago by actors.

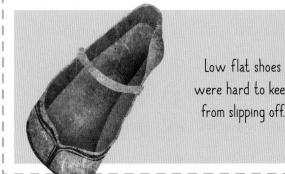

Low flat shoes were hard to keep from slipping off.

The poor had very simple shoes—sometimes, they used just a piece of fabric.

THE MIDDLE AGES	THE RENAISSANCE	THE BAROQUE	19TH CENTURY

Bows decorated both women's and men's shoes.

THE BAROQUE PERIOD

red heel to indicate exclusivity and noble status

Baroque shoes were decorated with embroidery and lace.

thin leather sole

Shoes with heels up to 4.5 inches long were worn by gentlemen and ladies.

The more decorations, the better!

They were all the rage with Baroque ladies, as well as with their chevaliers. Simply put, the 17th and 18th centuries were more than open to various ribbons, bows, laces, pearls, decorative clips, and alabaster. Noblemen and noblewomen would make themselves appear taller with **red heels**, which were becoming increasingly popular. Men advertised their masculinity with **high musketeer boots**, adorned with spurs and broad turn-ups. The highest boots would reach all the way up to your mid-thighs. And what did the destitute wear? What they always did—clogs or regular boots.

Baroque footwear became more and more comfortable.

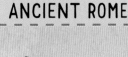

The cuffs of high leather boots—musketeers—was folded.

TIMELINE ⟶

| PREHISTORY | ANCIENT EGYPT | ANCIENT GREECE | ANCIENT ROME |

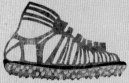

In the middle of the 19th century, ankle-high shoes fastened by a row of buttons were favored among women.

During the "century of steam," many different types of shoes came into being including elegant shoes, work shoes, and sports shoes.

The Steam Revolution

The 19th century removed the flashy red color from the heels and soles of noblemen's shoes. Nobility could afford higher-quality materials and design—that was the main difference between the rich and the poor. Elegant dandies would walk around in shoes made of **patent leather** or made with rubber straps. Unlike previous fashions, women's shoes reached up to the ankles, heels became much lower, and the fastening included buttons. The modern age also took footwear for children and athletes into account—the first baby and gym shoes were created.

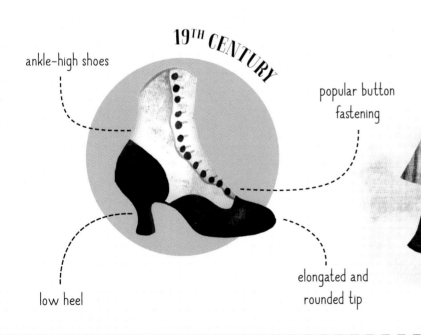

19ᵀᴴ CENTURY

ankle-high shoes

popular button fastening

low heel

elongated and rounded tip

 THE MIDDLE AGES | THE RENAISSANCE |  THE BAROQUE |  19ᵀᴴ CENTURY

Why tie shoes only with shoelaces?

Gideon Sundback
1880–1954

In the early 20th century, the Swedish inventor **Gideon Sundback** made some improvements to the slider, increased its lifespan, and started its successful career.

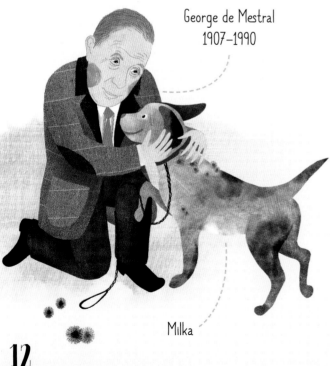

George de Mestral
1907–1990

Milka

Zippers

Why bother with laces when you can easily fasten your shoes with a zipper? Who do we have to thank for this change? How about **Elias Howe**, who came up with a sort of predecessor to the zipper, but wasn't very successful with it. In 1893, **Whitcomb Judson** came up with a similar zipper-based idea. His zipper had two rows of hooks which would get attached to one another by the slider. All one needed to do after the deed was done was put the slider in their pocket or closet, and that was it.

Elias Howe
1819–1867

Inspired by nature

Nature sometimes inspires scientists and inventors to come up with groundbreaking discoveries. And so it happened that the Swiss engineer **Georges de Mestral** stumbled on balls of thistle while walking his dog. Try removing thistle from animal fur—it stuck as if glued to it. While studying the system of clusters, the smart innovator noticed small hooks which fitted one another—he discovered Velcro. All of this occurred in the first half of the 20th century, and many years have passed since the walk and the zipper breakthrough, naturally. Since then, however, Velcro has been pretty busy.

Jindřich Waldes
1876–1941

Snap fasteners

The first snap fastener—**a two-piece metal snap button**—was most likely invented by former traveling businessman **Jindřich Waldes**. At any rate, what we do know is the name of the person who invented the groundbreaking machine to produce this fashionable metal article mechanically and sent it out into the world. The person was **Hynek Puc** and he did this in 1902.

Hynek Puc
1856–1938

Walter Hunt
1796–1859

Safety pins

If there's no other alternative, a safety pin is a good substitute for a button, zipper, or snap fastener. You might think that the person who came up with this practical idea was worth their weight in gold. Well, **Walter Hunt**, the American mechanic who invented it, was actually up to his ears in debt and couldn't pay it off. Luckily, a friend who once lent him some money had a heart of gold and the soul of a joker. He gave a piece of brass wire to the desperate Hunt and promised that if he'd make something useful out of it, he'd write the debt off and reward him to boot. And so Hunt thought and thought about it, bending the wire this way and that, until he made a **safety pin**. This was way back in 1849.

SKATES

THE ICE AGE

processed bone

It's freezing outside. Ponds are gleaming with ice. Awesome! Everyone, young and old, is tripping over themselves to go skating. They take their sharpened skates out of the closet, and off they go. Girls start doing pirouettes while boys turn into fierce hockey players, pushing the puck into the net with their hockey sticks. A few timid beginners fall down a couple of times and scrape their knees, but they become more and more assured of their skating skills by the end of the day. One must admit that the person who came up with such a fantastic thing as skates had a good head on their shoulders . . .

The ancient skater helped himself with a simple pole.

The oldest skates in the world

The oldest skates ever found were made around 3,000 BCE and were discovered at the bottom of a lake in Switzerland. Siberians made skates from walrus tusks, while the Chinese used bamboo.

The Ice Age is icy indeed

Let's go back to prehistoric times, specifically to the lands of frozen lakes and ponds. Back then, people had to travel long distances in search of food. **Walking on ice** was no fun, and so they had no choice but to sit down and think up the very first skates, which would make moving on frozen surfaces easier and faster. These prehistoric skates, made in the Stone Age, would later be discovered by archaeologists in Scandinavia, England, Hungary, Russia, and the Czech Republic.

TIMELINE ⟶

| 3,000 BCE | 4ᵀᴴ–3ᴿᴰ CENTURIES BCE | 15ᵀᴴ CENTURY |

Nothing better than iron!

A few centuries later—in the 4th and 3rd centuries BCE, to be precise—**Celts** started settling down in Europe, introducing their ability to work with iron. This skill not only benefitted farmers or warriors, but also greatly improved the concept of skates. How? Well, what do you think? Bones were replaced with iron, of course! An iron strip would be embedded into a wooden plate, and voilà! You could glide on the nearest pond, as fast as lightning. The earliest iron-made great-grandmother of our modern skates is almost 2,000 years old. Quite the timespan, huh?

processed bone

skates reconstructed by archeologists

THE 4TH–3RD CENTURY

metal buckles

leather straps

> The prehistoric model of skates was quite ahead of its time. In many regions, bone and wooden skates survived till the Middle Ages.

Jump in at the medieval end

Celtic-style skates were perfected and improved many times, up until the **Middle Ages**. Sure, the iron version was reserved for blue-blooded nobles while the peasants had no other option but to use bone skates. But at any rate, who cares? The point is that everyone could go skating. The most skillful even tried their hand at figure skating.

17TH CENTURY	19TH CENTURY	20TH CENTURY

SKATES

15

The design of the shoe was important as well.

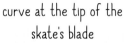

leathery decor

curve at the tip of the skate's blade

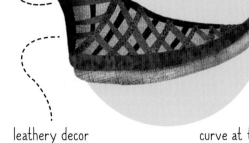

Dutch clog skates

Wanna skate? Put on your clogs!

In the Netherlands, **clogs** are the national footwear. It comes as no surprise, then, that the Dutch would even skate in them during medieval times. All they needed to do was attach an iron strip to the bottom, and off they went. At first, they needed to support themselves with poles because the edges of the iron strips weren't sharp enough, but as soon as a 15th-century Dutch apprentice woodworker figured out a way to sharpen the iron, other innovators followed, happily throwing their poles away and skating freely . . . as free as birds.

TIMELINE ⟶

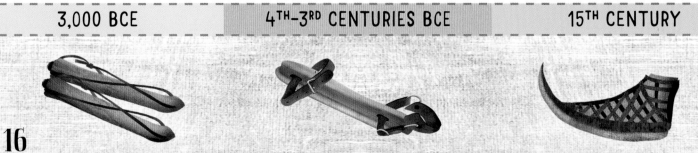

| 3,000 BCE | 4TH–3RD CENTURIES BCE | 15TH CENTURY |

16

The bendy end

The 15th century saw another significant innovation in skating—a distinct curve at the tip of the skate's blade. To be precise, even the first bone skates were a little bit curvy at the front due to the anatomical shape of the bones. But intentionally **curved tips** were a 100% guarantee that skaters wouldn't trip on an uneven surface or get stuck in a hole because of the sharp tip, breaking their nose in the process. And thirdly, let's allow our ancestors some vanity and finery, and consider the whole thing from the perspective of appearance. Wouldn't you agree that skates simply look better when their tips are curved?

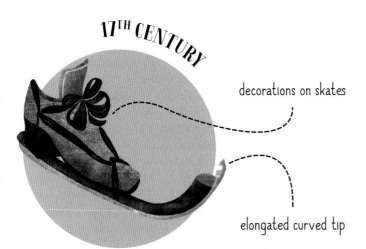

17TH CENTURY

decorations on skates

elongated curved tip

You can either go fast, or dance

As centuries went by, skates became increasingly popular. They were more and more accessible to the general public, and most importantly people greatly enjoyed using them! In the 17th century, **Emperor Rudolph II** held the first ever ice carnival at his royal court. And two centuries later, the first skating club was founded in Edinburgh, Scotland. At the same time, two types of skating began to be recognised—elegant figure skating, and adrenaline-filled speed skating.

17TH CENTURY   19TH CENTURY   20TH CENTURY

Jackson Haines

Cherchez le ballet

Born in the US, **Jackson Haines** was **a ballet dancer** through and through. And since he loved skates and skating, he decided to inject this sport with some of his dancing skills and ballet techniques. Words were soon followed by actions, and Jackson became the father of modern figure skating. When did this happen? The 19th century.

The blade tip is not yet connected to the shoe as in the 20th century version.

19TH CENTURY

leather shoe

Haines' dancing skate

Tiny teeth

In order for figure skaters to jump and do pirouettes, the 20th century saw tiny teeth being added to the blade tips of figure skates. And the past century brought another small innovation, too. Skate manufacturers elongated the blades and made them as thin as possible. This allowed skaters to spread their weight around and move faster. And to think that all this started during the Ice Age, with perpetually rumbling bellies and ordinary bones.

TIMELINE →

| 3,000 BCE | 4TH-3RD CENTURIES BCE | 15TH CENTURY |

Speed skaters use a different technique than ice skaters. The blade on speed skates does not have a curved tip. These skaters reach speeds of up to 25 miles per hour.

tip with toothed blade

sharpened blade

leather shoe with a heel

Contemporary skates allow skaters, when performing, to work perfectly with their center of gravity.

lace-up boot

| 17ᵀᴴ CENTURY | 19ᵀᴴ CENTURY | 20ᵀᴴ CENTURY |

SKATES

19

Equipment for sport lovers

Joseph Merlin
1735–1803

Roller skates

The first **roller skates** were introduced in 1760 when a masquerade was held in London. **Joseph Merlin**, a Belgian musician and inventor, built a pair of primitive roller skates for the occasion, intending to make a grand entrance while playing his violin. So he did. And because he had no idea how to brake to a halt, he hit a large mirror. Later in the 19th century, inventors of in-line and double-row skates vied with one another for patents. Some skates made it impossible to turn, others to brake. It wasn't until 1863, when a New Yorker named **Joseph Plimpton** came up with a pair of skates with a single row of four wheels, that it became possible to turn. It was these very skates that revolutionized the history of roller skating.

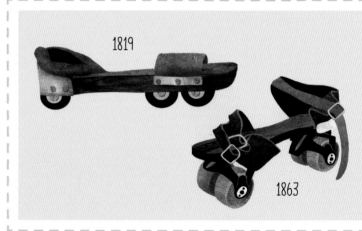

1819

1863

Skis

Just like skates, skis also originated in the Stone Age and for the same reason—to better move around regions covered in snow. The first prehistoric skis were actually **snowshoes** used to walk on snow. Over time, they changed and people started using them to sort of slide around. The skis allowed the user to travel, hunt, and fight comfortably, though they looked much different than the ones you can buy today. One ski—the take-off one—was shorter and its slide part was wrapped in fur. The slide surface of the longer ski was smooth. A single long pole was used for pushing off.

Skilled skiers could hunt while skiing.

The skater helped himself with a simple pole.

shorter take-off ski

basic long ski

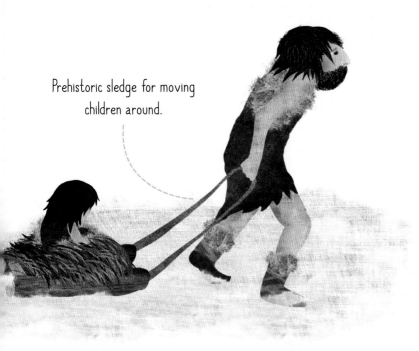

Prehistoric sledge for moving children around.

Sled

The oldest sled in the world was discovered by archeologists in **Heinola**, Finland. The date it was made? The impressive era of 6,500 BCE. As you can see, sleds and sledding have prehistoric origins. Originally, sleds appeared in regions which were covered in snow and ice for longs periods of time. That's as clear as a bell. Try traveling around snowy landscape with a wheeled wagon. One of the first people to use sled were Vikings and the indigenous inhabitants of northern Canada.

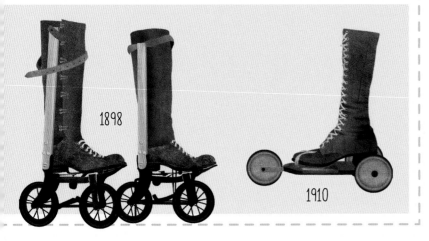

1898

1910

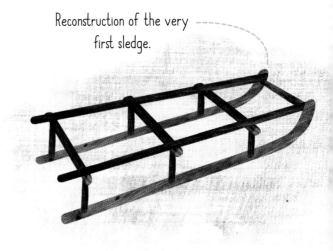

Reconstruction of the very first sledge.

Jump rope

Would you believe that jump ropes were probably favored as early as in Ancient China? They were also used by ancient Phoenicians, Egyptians, and Greeks. Playing with jump ropes was very popular in the Netherlands. Later, in the 17th century, the first Dutch immigrants introduced jump ropes in their new homeland—America. **The children of Dutch immigrants** would skip rope like crazy, and the locals would just shake their heads. What kind of oddity is this, to jump over one or two ropes while singing peculiar rhymes? A few centuries passed, and the jump rope is still in use—not only as part of children's games, but also of training programs for professional athletes. So get up and go skip some rope!

Everything your agile feet might need!

UMBRELLAS

In the beginning, there was a leaf and a scorching sun. The leaf turned into a parasol, the parasol into an umbrella. Today, people can choose any umbrella they want—women's, men's, children's, even dog's. Collapsible, non-collapsible, double, elegantly monochrome, colorful with coquettish lace, or nicely transparent and plastic. In brief, the immortal umbrellas have kept us company for centuries, regardless of whether it's raining cats and dogs or insanely hot.

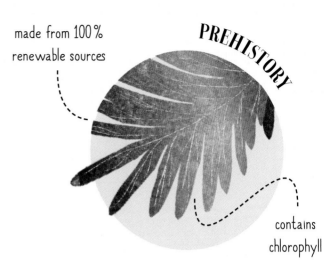

made from 100% renewable sources

PREHISTORY

contains chlorophyll

Oh boy, the sun is shining

Maybe it went something like this. Once upon a time, deep in the prehistoric era, our ancestors became annoyed with getting sunburnt from being exposed to direct sunlight all the time, and so they plucked **a large leaf**—a palm leaf, whenever possible—and hid themselves in its shade. The first primitive umbrella—or rather parasol—saw the light of day.

So you see—the original parasols were nothing but regular palm leaves that our distant ancestors, tired from the sun, held above their heads. The most inventive ones covered a pole with leather, and voilà! Even better protection from the sun—and possibly from the rain—became available. Today, we can use automatic umbrellas to shield ourselves from the harshest rain in an instant. But back then, the most reliable way to stay dry and not get a sunstroke was to hide in a safe cave or the wonderful shade of trees.

TIMELINE ⟶

PREHISTORY	ANCIENT EGYPT	ANCIENT CHINA

While anyone today can protect themselves with a parasol, back in antiquity this invention was used exclusively by the ruling class. Common Egyptians or Mesopotamians couldn't even think of owning such a luxury item, let alone actually own one. At the sites of all ancient civilizations and realms, archeologists stumble upon depictions of slaves who hold a parasol above the head of their master or mistress. Egyptian parasols, in fact, were giant fans made from the colorful feathers of beautiful birds.

Ancient Egypt

In Egypt, the sun would beat down upon people all day. The poor paid it no mind and worked their fingers to the bone. After all, they had no choice. The more fortunate among Egyptians—**the ruling class**—had a bunch of slaves fan them and hold parasols above their heads to make sure their skin would be as pale as possible.

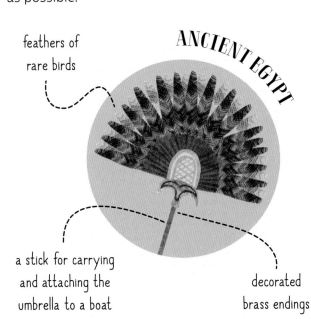

ANCIENT EGYPT

feathers of rare birds

a stick for carrying and attaching the umbrella to a boat

decorated brass endings

ANCIENT ROME

THE RENAISSANCE

18TH CENTURY

ANCIENT CHINA

Waxed paper provided great protection from the sun.

Bamboo was a favorite material of parasol manufacturers.

Put the umbrella down, please

Where did parasols start being folded? Probably in China, and it's not a recent invention, either—the original foldable parasol was invented about **2,000 years ago**!

The yellow parasol could only be owned by members of the royal family.

Keep the suntan away

Yes, you've read that correctly. While we want to be tan in modern times, ancient nobles emphasized their nobility by keeping their skin almost entirely **unblemished by the sun**. No wonder, then, that it was Ancient China specifically that virtually turned into a land of parasols. They started to be used about 4,000 years ago, and immediately became an important and indispensable fashion accessory, not to mention a symbol of wealth.

Originally, Chinese parasols were made out of silk and beautifully ornamented with traditional motifs—dragons, flowers, or scenes of nature. Around the 1st century BCE, silk was replaced with waxed paper. Back then, parasols symbolized power and nobility. In China and Japan, their length and color indicated the owner's social standing—with members of the royal family using red or yellow parasols while rich aristocrats made do with blue ones.

TIMELINE ⟶

PREHISTORY　　　　ANCIENT EGYPT　　　　ANCIENT CHINA

Send it to Europe!

By way of the Silk Road, of course—an important trade route. So that's what happened. While ladies in Ancient Greece took an immediate liking to **parasols**, brave men didn't. The scenario repeated itself further on, in Rome. Though once the parasol got there, it turned into **a real umbrella**!

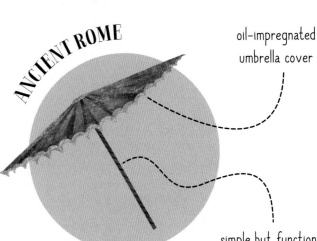

oil-impregnated umbrella cover

simple but functional

Roman parasols resemble Greek ones in appearance and structure.

Against the sun, against the rain

One day, shrewd Romans discovered that if they smeared some oil on the paper from the parasol's foldable screen, the whole thing would become **waterproof**—protecting them from rain. There's something beautiful about such simplicity, don't you think? And if one decided to attend gladiatorial combat in the amphitheater, they'd be well-advised to leave their umbrella or parasol at home. Who would be able to see over such a wall of umbrellas?

In Ancient Greece and Rome, noble ladies adored their parasols. And why wouldn't they? After all, these lavishly decorated screens prevented them from getting a highly undesirable tan. Parasols were also a symbol of their nobility, and thus an indispensable part of their wardrobe. Going out without a parasol? No woman or girl would ever think of committing such a faux pas.

ANCIENT ROME	THE RENAISSANCE	18TH CENTURY

The Renaissance

After ancient times umbrellas in European countries took a long break and weren't brought back until the progressive **Renaissance** rolled around. Sixteenth-century ladies used them to protect their faces from piercing sunlight, or to shield their elaborate hairdos from rain. Who'd want to look like a drowned rat, huh? While vain women expanded their collections of umbrellas and parasols in order to always have something to match their clothes, male fops were too tough for such accessories.

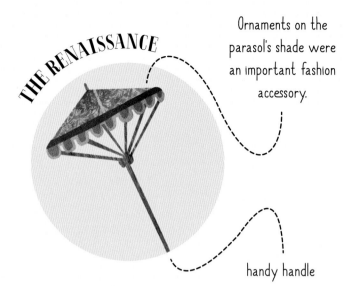

THE RENAISSANCE

Ornaments on the parasol's shade were an important fashion accessory.

handy handle

Twilight of the parasols

Renaissance, Baroque, Regency, and Romantic era ladies kept anxiously mindful of their pale and sun-beaten cheeks. They weren't going to be simple peasants. However, the beautifully tanned women of the 1920s caused parasols to retreat from fashion.

Baroque style   Romantic style   Regency style

TIMELINE →

| PREHISTORY | ANCIENT EGYPT | ANCIENT CHINA |

The bravest among the brave

Remember the name of this English gentleman. This 18th century daredevil didn't hold himself back and would stroll around London streets on rainy days, clutching an umbrella above his head. At first, passersby would cross the road in disgust rather than run into him, but over time they realized that it was no act of bravery to have rain pour down their collar. Thus, **Jonas Hanway** taught even the toughest of tough guys to carry an umbrella.

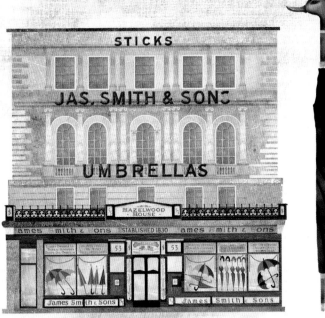

Practical umbrella for harsh men.

Jonas Hanway
1712–1786

An umbrella, m'lady?

Ding-a-ling! The bell above the shop's door rings and a young couple enters. The woman takes her gloves off and starts looking for a colorful umbrella, while the dishy guy who came with her wants his umbrella to be rendered in discreet shades of dark. It's the mid-19th century and we're in London, peeping into the first ever specialised umbrella shop. It's called **James Smith & Sons**.

ANCIENT ROME	THE RENAISSANCE	18TH CENTURY

Other practical things

Mr. Parkhaus

Wire hanger

Imagine that you have to always listen to your unhappy colleagues complain constantly that there's a lack of hooks to hang their jacket, coat, or windbreaker on. You'd be sick and tired of it in no time, right? **Mr. Parkhaus**, who lived in the early 20th century, certainly was. Luckily, he worked in a factory where different things were being made out of wire. One day in 1903, he simply ran out of patience, bent a wire, twisted it around firmly, and made a wire hanger.

Coat hanger

Presidents can do more than just preside over the country—take **Thomas Jefferson** (1743–1826). This Founding Father had enough time to do some light inventing when he wasn't too busy with politics. It was he who thought up the first ever coat hanger. Simply put, he refused to wear wrinkly jackets. So he built his own coat hanger. The next one didn't see the light of day until 1840 and was named after a famous French chocolate—the Etron. It had a beautiful carmine-red cover and a gilded hook. Why was it so fancy, you might wonder? Because it was a wedding gift for Queen Victoria and Albert, her fiancé.

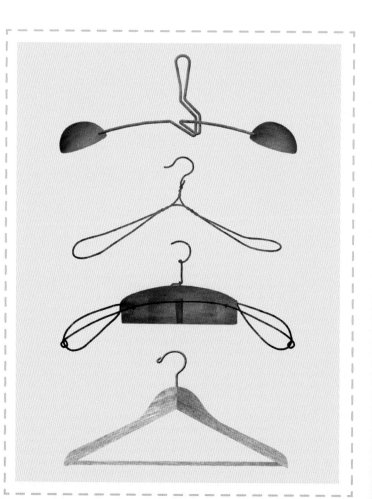

Bag

Throughout history, people have always needed something to put their stuff in. There were always some things they'd have to carry around. So what would they do? They'd make a small sack out of leather or reeds, attach a strap to it, and off they'd go, missing nothing. Sacks with a drawstring survived Antiquity and successfully held up until the Middle Ages. Then, they began to be replaced with leather, so-called **pittance bags** with long straps, often embellished with scenes from the Bible. Some time passed, and when the 17th century arrived, pittance bags turned into **bags with shoulder straps**—the ones we proudly wear to this day. Back then, they were mostly favored by farmers.

17th century bags were made from leather or cloth and had a long strap that could be easily worn over the shoulder. No wonder they were favored by pilgrims, craftsmen, as well as farmers!

Women's purses

Actual women's purses didn't appear until the **French Revolution**—or rather, until it introduced a new fashion trend. Wanting to emphasize their slim waists, the women refused to follow the traditions established by their predecessors and wear pouches under their skirts. But that didn't mean they intended to give up their perfumes or other knick-knacks! Thus, the first patterned and embroidered purses came to be, soon becoming an important fashion accessory.

Passenger luggage

The 19th century changed the world—which, naturally, included the way one traveled. People needed something practical so that they could pack their stuff, hop on a train, and go. And so passenger luggage came to be. Although . . . The very first example of passenger luggage was **a leather sack with a wooden frame** and back straps. It was made around **3,000 BCE** and was owned by a prehistoric man called **Ötzi**. Basically, it was one of the first backpacks ever created.

GLASSES

Some people are farsighted and need glasses. Meanwhile, others use them if they want to read or look at something close up. Even those who have eyes like a hawk will lose their perfect eyesight over time, and will have to wear glasses. But what's the history of this tool? Who was smart enough to have invented it?

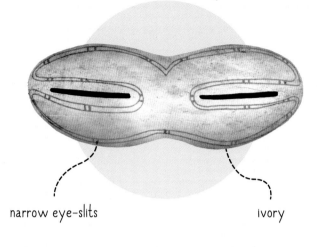

narrow eye-slits   ivory

Sun protection

Having poor eyesight was a huge problem if you happened to live in prehistoric times. "What should we do?" asked mammoth hunters. So they brewed herbal potions, performed shamanic healing rituals, and who knows what else—but nothing worked! The problem, you see, was that they didn't know about glasses, back then. Well, on the other hand, they did in a way! But their glasses only protected you from the **sunlight**. They were made from wood or ivory and looked like a mask or protective shield rather than the glasses we know today. Anyway, they served their purpose—so well, in fact, that the Inuit still wear them today.

potion healing eye infections

Later, our ancestors discovered something very interesting. When certain minerals and stones are shaped a certain way and used for observing distant objects, such objects appear closer or better-defined. As early as 4,000 years ago, the first scholars who suffered from poor eyesight resorted to transparent semiprecious stones to read better. But let's be honest—it was nothing to write home about.

TIMELINE ⟶

| PREHISTORY | ANCIENT EGYPT | ANCIENT ROME | ANCIENT CHINA |

30

Is this the first lens?

Ancient Egyptians were brilliant, indeed. Not only did they manage to build the breath-taking pyramids we admire today, but they could also blow glass and shape it in different ways. No wonder, then, that the **very first crystal lens**—made in 2,000 BCE—originated in Egypt.

Egyptian with a crystal lens.

emerald lens

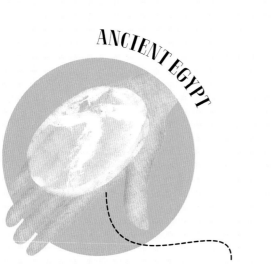

ANCIENT EGYPT

The oldest lens in the world.

The educated antiquity

Yes, ancient scholars suffered from worsening eye-sight, too, and since they wanted to live a full life instead of having to constantly rely on their slaves, they had to find a solution. **Seneca**, a famous Greek philosopher, found out that if he filled a glass ball with water and placed it on the top of the page he was reading, the letters seemed bigger and he could work in peace. In this way, he devoured any book that fell into his hands.

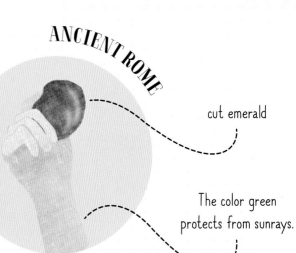

ANCIENT ROME

cut emerald

The color green protects from sunrays.

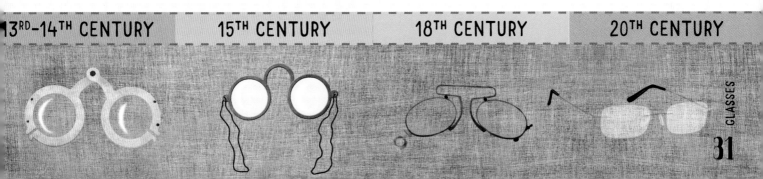

13RD–14TH CENTURY   15TH CENTURY   18TH CENTURY   20TH CENTURY

GLASSES

Cut lenses were appreciated by Chinese scholars.

Reading stones

While Marco Polo, a famous explorer, is traveling through China, he can't help but notice that Chinese sages use lenses made from cut **glass** or **crystal** in order to read better, simply by placing the lens on the text, flat side down. This was one of the few things that China didn't come up with before Europeans. European scholars knew of this method of making letters seem larger as early as 1,000 AD, and used it frequently. They even pulled a chain through the glass and wore it around their neck.

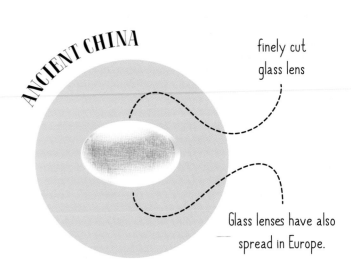

ANCIENT CHINA

finely cut glass lens

Glass lenses have also spread in Europe.

Cut crystal lenses were a brilliant tool that made reading easier for everyone with poor vision. But there was a significant drawback—you had to constantly hold them in your hand. So people were forced to find a more comfortable solution—glasses, which rested on your nose.

The first manufacturer

Guess who? A monk named **Alexander Spinosa**, who was allegedly kindhearted enough to produce glasses for his monk friends at the turn of the 14th century. They were simple and didn't have any arms—or earpieces—meaning that readers had to hold them in front of their eyes. Originally, they even had no rims. For the first spectacles, rims used such materials as bones, iron, turtle shells, silver, gold, or leather. It's no surprise that the first manufacturer was a monk. After all, monks and scholars were the ones who needed glasses the most at the time. It wasn't until the printing press was invented around 1440 that readerships grew, and so did the demand for glasses.

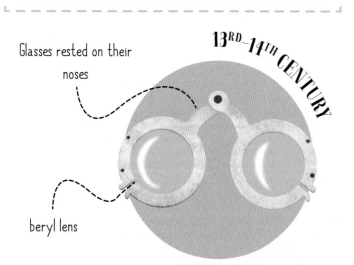

Glasses rested on their noses

13RD–14TH CENTURY

beryl lens

TIMELINE →

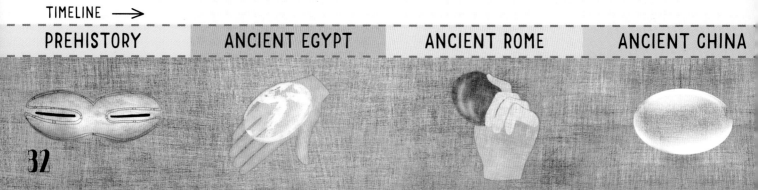

PREHISTORY | ANCIENT EGYPT | ANCIENT ROME | ANCIENT CHINA

Keeping the glasses in place

This was a problem faced by brainy people who lived before and during the Renaissance. Having to hold your glasses while reading wasn't exactly comfortable, you know? And so the 15th and 16th century introduced: glasses **attached to one's hat**; glasses **attached to one's nose** with a clip (ouch, it hurts!); glasses **tied to one's head** with strings; and last but not least, glasses whose laces ran over the reader's ears and were weighted at the end. Quite funny, don't you think?

A judge hiding his eyes behind dark lenses.

Alexander Spinosa

The Chinese, especially judges, wore glasses which consisted of thin plates made from gray quartz. Meaning, you couldn't see the wearer's eyes at all. No, this wasn't because of vanity, but to meet the needs of the profession. Those working in the Chinese justice system needed to seem as mysterious as possible, and glasses prevented criminals from looking into their eyes and guessing what they were thinking.

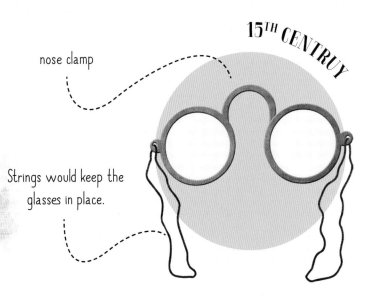

15ᵀᴴ CENTRUY

nose clamp

Strings would keep the glasses in place.

3ᴿᴰ–14ᵀᴴ CENTURY   15ᵀᴴ CENTURY   18ᵀᴴ CENTURY   20ᵀᴴ CENTURY

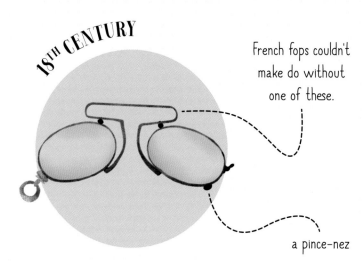

French fops couldn't make do without one of these.

a pince-nez

Great monocle, wouldn't you say?

Vanity eyewear

By the end of the 18th century, gentlemen grew to love the so-called **monocle**—glasses with a single lens that rested against their brow ridge and was held in place by their facial muscles. Meanwhile, ladies swaggered around with so-called **lorgnons**—two connected eyepieces with a handle. And in France, people wore a **pince-nez**—glasses with a clip.

A lorgnette for true ladies.

In the 18th century, tinted glasses weren't very popular among our ancestors. For some reason, they though they weren't attractive and wore them only rarely.

TIMELINE ➞

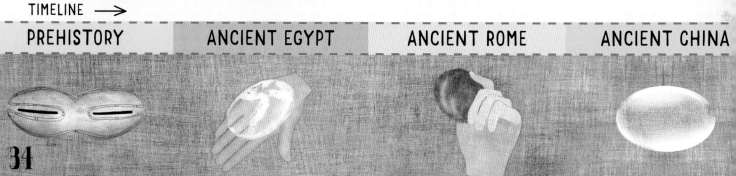

| PREHISTORY | ANCIENT EGYPT | ANCIENT ROME | ANCIENT CHINA |

Comfortable glasses

Comfortable glasses with **anatomically shaped earpieces** didn't start being produced until the early 20th century—phew. And hurray! Can you imagine playing football while wearing a lorgnon, or tag while a pince-nez is bouncing up and down on your nose? I certainly can't.

Such earpieces don't hurt behind your ears.

These glasses are super comfortable.

A kid wearing one of the first comfortable glasses.

The uncomfortable Middle Ages made sharp head movements impossible as the glasses would immediately fall of.

The 15th century introduced earpieces, but those who had to wear glasses still weren't fully satisfied.

Modern, anatomically shaped glasses stick to your nose as if glued there.

13ᴿᴰ–14ᵀᴴ CENTURY · · · 15ᵀᴴ CENTURY · · · 18ᵀᴴ CENTURY · · · 20ᵀᴴ CENTURY

GLASSES

35

With or without glasses?

Ann Sheridan
1940

Sunglasses

We already know that brave prehistoric hunters protected their eyesight from sharp sunlight by wearing bone masks with narrow slits for eyes. Later, when the Roman Empire rolled around, the famous Emperor Nero would watch gladiatorial matches through a green emerald that was supposed to absorb harmful sunrays. Actual sunglasses were invented in the 18th century. The dark magnifying glass, set in bone rims, was considered an unsightly medical aid rather than a fashion accessory. As soon as **movie stars** put on sunglasses, though, people went ballistic.

Ski goggles

The first ever ski goggles resembled the very first sunglasses. They, too, protected the original Inuit ancestors from snow blindness. The Inuit carved them out of reindeer bones, wood, or shells, and attached them to their faces with reindeer tendons. **Robert Smith**, a dentist who specialised in braces, loved to ski and did so whenever he could. No wonder, then, that it was **he and his wife** who created the very first modern ski goggles in **1965**.

High-quality protection that leads to high performance on the slopes.

Contact lenses

Being able to see without wearing glasses . . . by putting a lens directly on your eye. In the past, great inventors pursued this line of thinking, too, chief among them the brilliant inventor Leonardo da Vinci. The groundbreaking discovery didn't arrive until the 20th century, when a professor made it. **Otto Wichterle** had long racked his brain over making a lens out of **hydrophilic gels** that would be suitable for the human eye. And then Christmas of 1961 came along—and with it a building kit called Merkur, from which Mr. Wichterle was finally able to construct the very first lens machine.

Swimming goggles

Would you believe that swimming goggles originated as far back as the 14th century? Back then, **Persian pearl hunters** protected their eyes with masks that were made from turtle shell and polished so much they turned transparent. The divers' eyes were protected by an air bubble inside the goggles, allowing them to see underwater. In 1911, **Thomas Burgess** swam across the English Channel. To protect his eyes, he put **regular motorcycle goggles** on. Yes, they did let some water in if he dove under the surface, but they helped quite a lot with swimming. In 1916, the first actual waterproof swimming glasses were patented. Their inventor? **C. P. Troppman**.

The first swimming goggles, by C. P. Troppman

Swimmer with waterproof swimming goggles

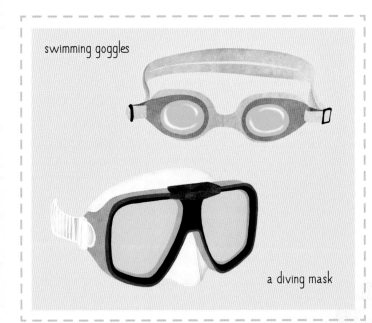

swimming goggles

a diving mask

DOLLS

When a small girl has a birthday, guess what she gets? A doll most likely, several of them if she's lucky. Girls' bedrooms are stuffed with long-haired figures, babies, princesses, and stuffed animals. Some of them stare at the wall, while others throw conspiratorial looks at the world. Some talk, others weep, and there are yet other ones who can pee themselves on command. Happy owners pamper their dolls, dress and comb them, or wheel them around in their own little carriages. But how did girls play in the ancient times, anyway? Did our great-great-great-great grandmothers have dolls as well?

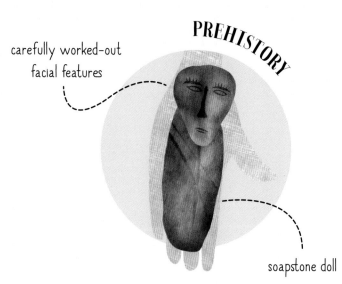

PREHISTORY

carefully worked-out facial features

soapstone doll

Prehistoric dolls?

In prehistoric times, children didn't exactly have loads of time to play. Well, you know, they were mostly preoccupied with surviving back then, and were lucky if they lived to see another day. There was danger lurking everywhere and one had to constantly help the adults find something to eat. Despite this, prehistoric children did indeed play, as a small doll from the **Bronze Age** proves, for example. It was discovered by archeologists in Siberia, in a child's grave. The doll was made from talc—a greasy stone—and has a distinct face.

Apart from dolls, children also liked animal figures. For example, wooden crocodiles were particularly favored in Ancient Egypt.

TIMELINE ⟶

| PREHISTORY | ANCIENT EGYPT | ANCIENT GREECE | 14TH–15TH CENTURY |

Long live the mummy!

In Ancient Egypt, children played with dolls, too. Parents would carve the **toys from wood**, shape them from the **mud of the fertile Nile**, or sew them **from pieces of cloth**. Such dolls could come with their own equipment, houses, or animal herds. Toys in the shape of mummies and sarcophagi were no rarity, either. It all depended on how skillful the parent and children were. The poorest of the poor made do with ordinary sticks.

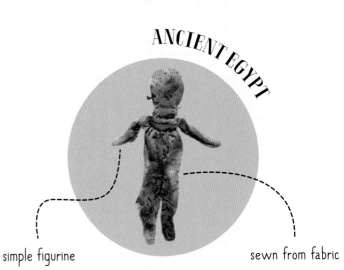

ANCIENT EGYPT

simple figurine

sewn from fabric

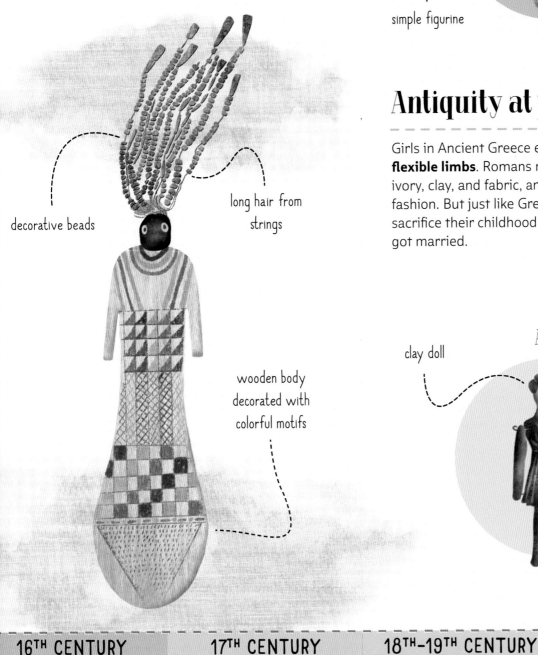

decorative beads

long hair from strings

wooden body decorated with colorful motifs

Antiquity at play

Girls in Ancient Greece enjoyed dolls with moving, **flexible limbs**. Romans made their dolls from wood, ivory, clay, and fabric, and dressed them in the latest fashion. But just like Greek girls, Romans had to sacrifice their childhood dolls to the gods once they got married.

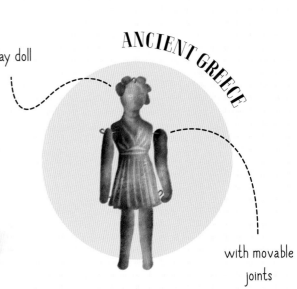

clay doll

ANCIENT GREECE

with movable joints

| 16TH CENTURY | 17TH CENTURY | 18TH–19TH CENTURY | 20TH CENTURY |

a clay horse

Kruseler dolls

The Middle Ages

Medieval dolls were sometimes made from wood, but mostly from potter's clay. The wealthier the family, the more elaborate and better equipped the doll. The figurines were usually dressed in regular worldly clothes. Some wore a scarf the maker created for them, a so-called **Kruseler**. Such dolls were all the rage in the 14th and 15th centuries. Apart from them, the Middle Ages also had figurines of knights, monks, and Madonnas on offer.

a model of a favorite wax doll

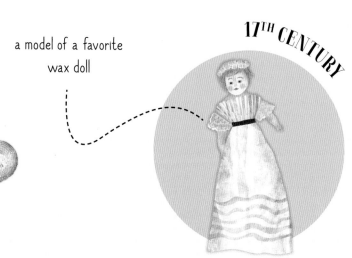

17ᵀᴴ CENTURY

TIMELINE ⟶

PREHISTORY	ANCIENT EGYPT	ANCIENT GREECE	14ᵀᴴ–15ᵀᴴ CENTURY

A little bit of fashion and wood

Sixteenth-century French Renaissance dolls could boast the same clothes the mothers of their owners wore. There's a reason why France is the world's leader in fashion. Meanwhile at around the same time, Germans and the Dutch started making **wooden figurines with joints**. They were sold naked so that children could sew the clothing themselves, reflecting their vision and skills.

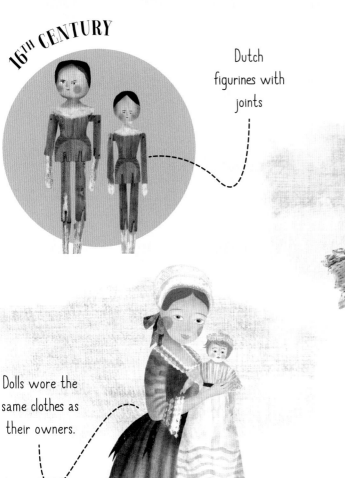

16TH CENTURY

Dutch figurines with joints

Dolls wore the same clothes as their owners.

Waxy beauty

In the 17th century, Italy expanded the trend of **wax dolls** into Germany. Girls were obsessed with them back then. And who wouldn't be! Those dolls wouldn't wear anything that wasn't a rare noblewoman's gown. But they didn't experience the height of fame until Great Britain adopted them. They had slim bodies and light hair made from real human hair.

Green or blue

Throughout the 18th century, dolls were usually made from wood. In the 19th century, though, dolls with beautiful **porcelain heads**, proudly sitting atop leather or cloth bodies, began to be in demand. Until the Victorian era rolled around, every single doll had brown glassy eyes, but thanks to **Queen Victoria**, the world of doll fashion experienced a trend of sky-blue eyes at the beginning of the 19th century.

One drawback of the porcelain heads was that they were easy to break.

18ᵀᴴ–19ᵀᴴ CENTURY

sky-blue eyes

Doll's bodies were made from leather and cloth.

fragile porcelain head

I'm a doll. Who's more?

The 19th century was very good with dolls. The French ones especially, intended for wealthy girls, were a leading voice in fashion. The German ones were cheaper, but no less beautiful, and therefore flooded the market. The invention of paper dolls that could be dressed also proved to be popular—almost all girls had them, dressing and undressing them, adorning and cutting new shapes constantly.

Ragdolls

While little girls from wealthy families could boast dolls that were almost indistinguishable from them—their owners—poor girls usually had to make do with **rag dolls**, one of the reasons being that it was easy to make such a doll at home. The rag has always been an available material—no wonder that fabric or rag dolls are the oldest, historically speaking. Rag dolls are soft, nice to hold in your arms, and don't weigh much—even toddlers find them easy to carry around. So there's your answer to why it's these soft fabric dolls that have been the most favored by girls across centuries while dolls with porcelain heads were erased from history.

TIMELINE ⟶

| PREHISTORY | ANCIENT EGYPT | ANCIENT GREECE | 14ᵀᴴ–15ᵀᴴ CENTURY |

Celluloid is only for films?

Oh no, celluloid isn't just **a film-making material**. In the 20th century, dolls were created from it as well. This synthetic material made them much cheaper than the porcelain ones, and therefore more readily accessible to everyone. But uh-oh! The celluloid little girls were much easier to destroy than the regular versions. Fortunately, the 20th century introduced many new artificial materials, this time indestructible kinds.

Modern dolls can walk and even take a poop.

a baby doll

20ᵀᴴ CENTURY

This doll is nearly indistinguishable from an actual baby.

They can do anything

At the dawn of toy-making, a doll was just a thin stick dressed in a leaf you'd pluck from a tree. As time went by, dolls became shaped in more beautiful and elaborate ways. New functions were added, too. Now, no girl bats an eye at a doll that shakes her head from side to side, weeps, eats porridge, walks, crawls, gurgles, laughs, talks, sings, or even repeats entire words and sentences its mom says. What would prehistoric girls, with their clothed sticks, think about such dolls? At any rate, stick dolls have one thing in common with today's ultra-modern dolls—they show little girls what it's like to be a mom and take care of a baby.

16ᵀᴴ CENTURY   17ᵀᴴ CENTURY   18ᵀᴴ–19ᵀᴴ CENTURY   20ᵀᴴ CENTURY

DOLLS

43

Enter the kingdom of children

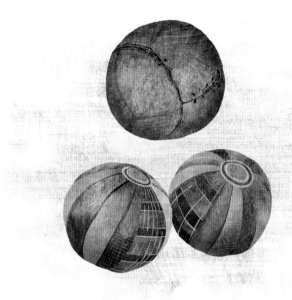

Margarete Steiff

Teddy bears for every bed

Moms have been sewing cloth figurines for their children since time immemorial. But the first ever teddy bear didn't see the light of day until the end of the 19th century. It was made by **Margarete Steiff**, a German seamstress, using a pattern created by Richard Steiff, her nephew, who decided to create a brown teddy bear as a boy's version of the doll. At the beginning of the 20th century, this 20-inch-tall bear with a waxy muzzle started appearing in shops and children's bedrooms. The oldest ones—the original teddy bears—resembled their living counterparts due to their short foreheads and longish muzzles.

Pacifiers

Even Ancient Egyptians sucked on pacifiers as tiny babies. To be precise, they were more like **suction cups** with no milk in them. Later, ancient babies sucked on **special animal toys** with holes in their faces. From these holes, sweet honey would seep into the infant's tiny mouth. Medieval babes used **cloth knots.** Pacifiers didn't start looking the way we think of them today until the 19th century. Dyes were expensive back then, and so the only pacifiers on offer were black, white, or chestnut brown.

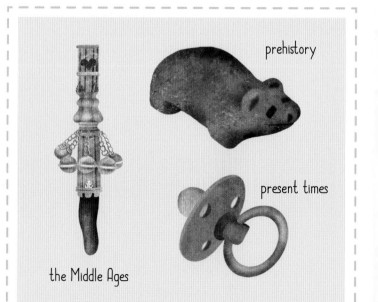

prehistory

present times

the Middle Ages

Balls

Once again, this may surprise you but balls are depicted on some images made as early as **Ancient Egypt**. Later in Greece, athletes used balls for different workouts. Romans went further still with their five types of balls. They played with small balls, medium-sized ones, large, largest, and empty ones. Leather or various fabrics—that's what went into making this round equipment over the course of human history. But **pig bladders** were definitely the most bizarre material ever used. Such balls were owned by boys in 16th-century England. Does this sound weird? Oh, come on, wait till you hear that the balls were wrapped in pigskin so that it wouldn't be easy to kick a hole into them.

prehistory

19th century

Antiquity

the Middle Ages

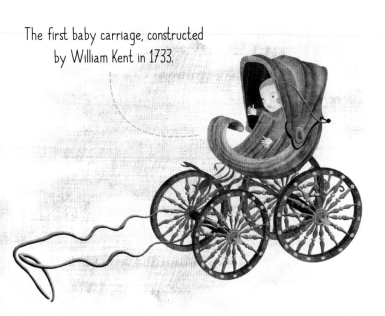

The first baby carriage, constructed by William Kent in 1733.

Rattles

Rattles, owned pretty much by all toddlers everywhere, originated deep in prehistoric times. That's because these toys offered not only a long night of uninterrupted sleep, but also **protection from evil spirits**. Back then, people believed that the sound would chase all bad creatures away from the baby. As time went by, rattles became more beautiful and elaborate. No wonder, then, that rich toddlers in medieval and modern times could play with silver, golden, or pearl rattles.

Baby carriages

Moms have needed some way to transport their babies since time immemorial. And so they carried them in scarves, hand baskets, pack baskets, or portable cradles. And because kids tend to get heavy as they grow up, parents would sit them down on wheeled stools. This was in the 5th century BCE, in Asia. The first real carriage was constructed in the 18th century by **William Kent**, a landscape architect, and was meant for the children of the Duke of Devonshire. It looked like a small chariot, and a pony or goat would be harnessed to it.

present time

PERFUME

Wow, what's that wonderful scent? Can you smell it? It's like a blooming meadow, or soap boiled with love. Whenever women get ready for a ball, a party, or just to go out, they put on some perfume, stored in an ornate little vial, sparkling beautifully—a blue spark here, a green spark there, translucent or sweetly pink. But what did the first perfume look like? And who was the first woman to use it?

a blend of herbal essences inside

a container that pleased every woman

Mesopotamia

Sumerian women wanted Sumerian men to like them, to find them nice-smelling. That's why they added **herbal essences** into their baths, made from jasmine, hyacinth, or cedar, and carefully rubbed them into their skin and hair . . . to smell nice, oh so nice.

> The year is 2,000 BC. Mesopotamia boasts the first chemical factory and pharmacy in the world. Among other things, it produces perfumes—who would have thought? At the same time, opulent women in Pyrga, Cyprus, could also enjoy great scents.

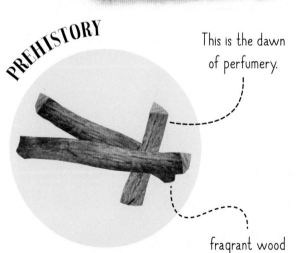

PREHISTORY

This is the dawn of perfumery.

fragrant wood

Fragrant wood

Some types of wood smell really nice when thrown into fire. Our ancestors noticed this in the times of mammoth-chasing and hunting. So that's one answer down—**per fumum** = to smoke through.

TIMELINE ⟶

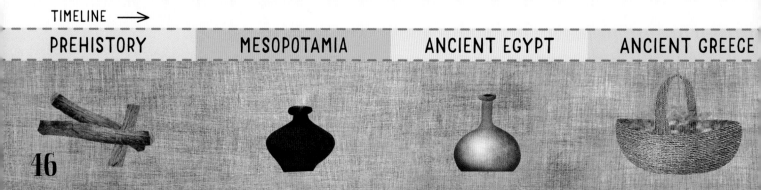

| PREHISTORY | MESOPOTAMIA | ANCIENT EGYPT | ANCIENT GREECE |

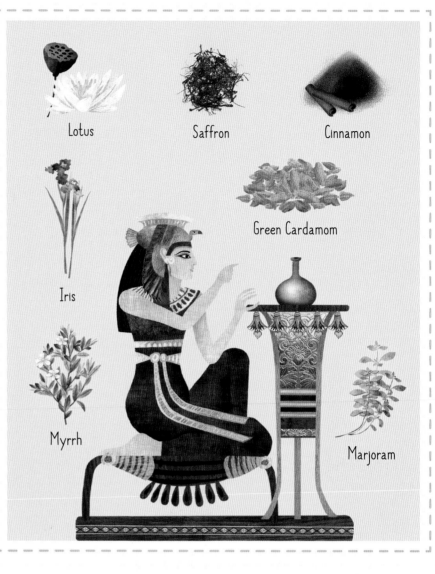

Lotus

Saffron

Cinnamon

Green Cardamom

Iris

Myrrh

Marjoram

Tapputi–a perfume-maker from Babylonia

7 herbs

In Ancient Egypt, the production of essential oils was the prerogative of priests. Each god and each season was assigned its own smell. Myrrh, cinnamon, lotus, saffron, cardamom, marjoram, and iris—these **7 herbs** formed the basis of **Queen Cleopatra's** most favorite perfume. Whenever the proud ruler set off on an overseas voyage, the sails of her boat had to be soaked in rose water. Wherever she sailed, the smell followed . . .

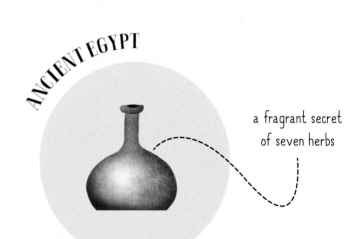

ANCIENT EGYPT

a fragrant secret of seven herbs

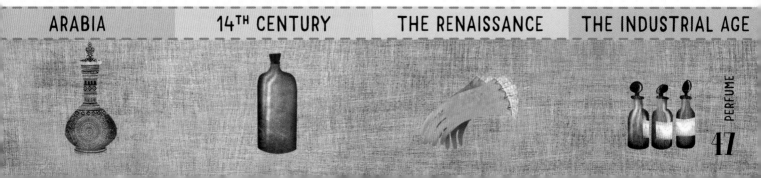

ARABIA   14TH CENTURY   THE RENAISSANCE   THE INDUSTRIAL AGE

Oh, that puppy smells nice

Greeks, believe it or not, actually competed with one another to see who could be doused in the most perfume. Each part of their body was perfumed with a different scent, and there was no lack of options—lily, lavender, myrtle, violet, marjoram, and iris. Whenever noble guests attended splendid feasts, servants sprinkled them with fragrant flowers. Even **the dogs** that were allowed to lie between the couches and tables **had to be scented**.

Hungarian alchemical workshop

ANCIENT GREECE

a basket full of fragrant blossoms

Hungarian Water

It's the 14th century, and we're in Hungary, at Queen Elizabeth of Poland's court. The court alchemist is experimenting with rosemary and saffron, and voilà! The first real perfume ever produced in Europe is here! We'll call it **Hungarian water**. And the name of this skilled alchemist? It has vanished into oblivion.

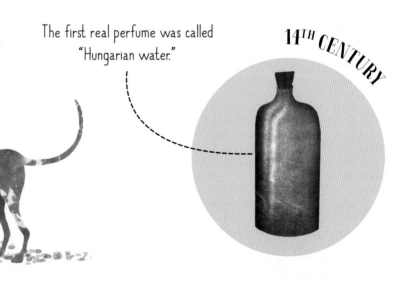

The first real perfume was called "Hungarian water."

14TH CENTURY

TIMELINE →

PREHISTORY	MESOPOTAMIA	ANCIENT EGYPT	ANCIENT GREECE

What preceded Hungarian water

It's the 10th century, and Arabs have just invented **the distilling apparatus**. Perfume production is about to get wild! Roses are being grown in huge fields, to be later used for rose oil. Perfumers discover new aromatic plants, and are constantly coming up with new and unusual scents to pamper people's noses with enjoyment. The Arab city of Bagdad even becomes the hub of perfume producers.

supreme Arabic utility design of the 10th century

ARABIA

an ornamented flacon with an oriental perfume

Thank the Crusaders

Fearless knights brought vials of irresistible scents from their journeys and gave them to their wives and mistresses. That's how the first perfumes, desired by women rich and poor, **reached Europe**.

Any perfume has three parts:
1. Top/Head notes—the scent you notice first.
2. Middle/heart notes—the scent that's released once the head fades away.
3. Base notes—soft whiffs of scent that can linger for up to several hours.

Catherine de' Medici

Gloves and perfumes go perfectly together. No wonder, then, that glove and perfume makers established a joint guild. After all, gloves needed to be scented in order for the smell of leather to be covered.

Galimard, a French glove maker, was the first one to ever perfume leather gloves.

Lavender extract was the very first substance used for perfuming gloves.

THE RENAISSANCE

ornamental lace

Renaissance

Catherine de' Medici, an Italian woman who married Henry II of France, wanted to smell nice. She was inspired by the lavender meadows and rose bushes that grew near the city of **Grasse**. In the blink of an eye, a perfume plant was set up, fired up, and ready to go. The **art of scent-making** permanently moved there, to France.

TIMELINE ⟶

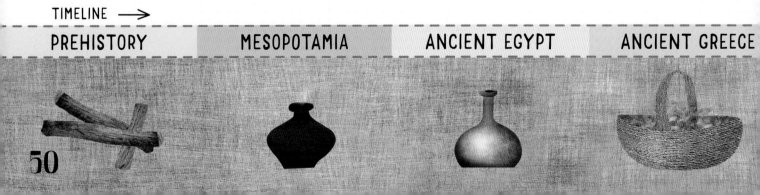

PREHISTORY   MESOPOTAMIA   ANCIENT EGYPT   ANCIENT GREECE

Special caps prevented the aroma from escaping.

Common bottles containing uncommon smells

The Industrial Age

Among other things, the Industrial Revolution contributed to the invention of fragrant essences. The scent of perfumes stopped being dependent on the plantations, which grew herbs and aromatic plants. All one needed was **a well-equipped chemistry lab**, a good head on their shoulders, and a refined nose.

Chanel No. 5

The legendary perfume invented by **Coco Chanel**, a famous French designer, smelled of soap, lemons, cherry blossoms, and flowers, not to mention her poor childhood, spent in an orphanage.

the famous Coco Chanel

N°5
CHANEL
PARIS

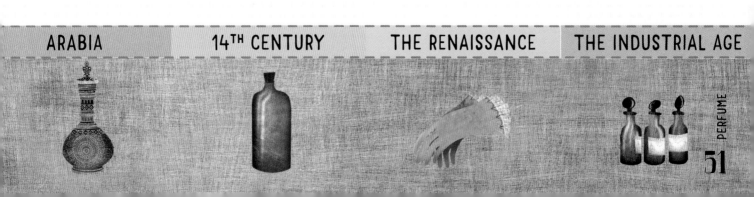

What you can find in the bathroom

Hans Schwarzkopf

Schwarzkopf shampoo

Shampoo

Champo—an Indian-English term which means "to knead". When a person washes their hair, they're actually furiously kneading it. In ancient times, people used to wash their hair with soap. The result? Nothing to write home about. Hair simply needs something much better—for example some aromatic herbs, which people did add to soaps.
Do you know the name **Hans Schwarzkopf**? In 1904, he came up with the first real shampoo, one based on powder and soluble in water. A few years passed, and things took a quick turn. The shampoo powder was stuffed into tubes, and the era of hair cosmetics kicked off with a bang.

Modern **conditioners** are nothing new under the sun. They're basically the same thing as the plant oils that women and men have been rubbing into their hair ever since Antiquity.

Combs

Combing your hair is another part of maintaining good hygiene. Even our ancient ancestors used simple combs, made from bones, wood, or animal horns. In prehistoric times, people would decorate them with engraved scenes of war, while people in Antiquity preferred pearls. Medieval ivory combs were adorned with pictures of flowers or with religious motifs. Comb your hair before entering a church, the custom went, and many towns and villages had a shared **comb for all**.

a medieval comb

a prehistoric comb

a present-day comb

Make-up

Even Ancient Egyptians used lipstick to make themselves appear more beautiful. There wasn't anything they weren't willing to do for beauty! And so whenever they wanted their lips to be violet, they didn't hesitate and reached for makeup containing toxic substances. If they preferred their lips to be red, then to heck with it! Who would care that the **red lipstick** consisted of crushed carmine beetles? The Middle Ages didn't look kindly on female beauty, but the 20th century and its movie stars brought lipstick back into the spotlight.

Marilyn Monroe

Nefertiti

lipstick

eyeshadow

Soap

soap portioning

Good **hygiene** is the cornerstone of good health—any small child knows that. And you can't have good hygiene without soap. Ancient nations solved this conundrum by washing themselves in aromatic oils. The Middle Ages cobbled up a soap made from ashes and fats—beef tallow or olive oil, if one lived in the sunny regions of Southern Europe. The 19th century came up with **soaps cut into cubes**—not luxury items by any means, just a strange brown goo that a shopkeeper would weigh out for you. Luckily, we live in the 21st century, where we're spoiled for choice.

HORSE TOYS

When a person is born, their mom rocks them in her arms, back and forth, back and forth, so that the tiny baby feels nice and loved. Whenever the little human doesn't like something, it starts crying so that the pair of kind hands takes it and once again begins rocking it back and forth. Rocking is simply fun and soothing. No wonder, then, that the first ever rocking toys included a rocking horse.

ANTIQUITY

clay decorated with ornament

a toy from Ancient Greece, around 950–900 BCE

horse on a stick—a toy favored by our ancestors

Antiquity and animals

Children probably played with **animal models** as early as prehistoric times. Simply put, humanity has been surrounded by animals from time immemorial. Since horses are creatures that can be easily ridden, making the world appear smaller as a result, it's no surprise that children could already play with wheeled models of horses in 500 BCE. Ancient Greeks favored a wooden horse head on a stick—a small boy would sit astride the stick, and bam! Off he went to an imaginary battle, or to go on an ordinary ride. This toy remained popular later, too—in the Middle Ages. Well, you know, knights had to be taught from an early age.

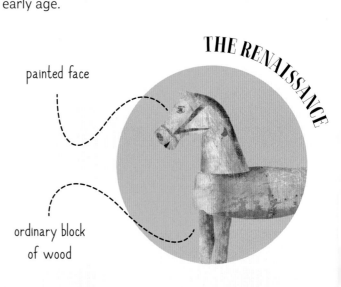

THE RENAISSANCE

painted face

ordinary block of wood

TIMELINE ⟶

ANTIQUITY	THE RENAISSANCE	17TH CENTURY

Toy horses

During the Renaissance, toy horses had a log for the body, four legs, and a roughly shaped head at one end of the body. Such horses made for **an excellent ride**, though they didn't yet rock. Rocking in the horse saddle didn't come until one hundred years later, in the 17th century, when the toy's legs were supplemented with curved boards. When was this rocking toy first made? And who thought it up? We'll probably never know.

Original rocking horses were made—surprise, surprise—from wood. As time went by, manufacturers started using other materials as well. And so, they began making rocking horses from leather, with genuine horsehair, textiles, even metal. The sky was the limit. Later, children could enjoy not only rocking horses, but other animals, too. For example, roosters were a favorite toy of choice.

The oldest rocker

One of the oldest surviving **rocking horses** comes from 1610. It likely belonged to the English king, **Charles I.** You'd be hard-pressed to find such a neat toy in poor families, you know? Mostly, it could be found among high-status, wealthy classes. Frequently, it was a perfect show of craftsmanship and artistry, a faithful copy of actual horse breeds.

17TH CENTURY

the oldest rocking horse

It belonged to the future King of England—Charles I

18TH CENTURY   19TH CENTURY   20TH CENTURY

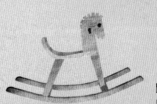

lush mane

18TH CENTURY

artwork
of a living horse

I want a horse, too

No exaggeration, the 18th century adored its rocking horses. There wasn't a single wealthy family who didn't own one. Both girls and boys used them to prepare for riding actual physical animals. At first, rocking horses were **unstable** and **relatively heavy**, but as the 18th century went on, they became lighter and more elegant.

Another royal horse

Feast your eyes! This fantastic little horse first saw the light of day sometime around 1750. It was made for the future king of Sweden, **Prince Gustav III**, and the manufacturers truly gave it their all. The mighty steed even had a leather saddle and actual reins.

Children have loved
rocking horses for ages.

As a child, Gustav III of Sweden owned a luxury rocking horse that was painted gray-and-white and reared up on an elaborately decorated gilded pedestal that doubled as a rocker. No one but the future ruler himself was allowed to mount such a rare steed.

TIMELINE →

ANTIQUITY	THE RENAISSANCE	17TH CENTURY

This type of rocking horse was safe.

The safest version

In the 19th century, the production of rocking horses moved from small workshops to **factories**—that's how great the demand was. From Great Britain—the likely cradle of rocking horses—this toy spread all over Europe, earning much success. All children wanted to have their own horse! At the end of the 19th century, a couple of innovations made sure that the rocking horse would no longer move around the room when rocked, but simply and safely sway back and forth at a single place. Hurray, let's get on! Parents needn't worry.

draft patent for an improved rocking horse

19TH CENTURY

detail of the safe structure

To arms!

During WWI, the production of rocking horses slowly dwindled. Who would think about playing when there's a war going on? Skilled craftsmen had to switch to manufacturing weapons. Later in the 20th century, though, rocking horses were made from **wood**, **metal**, even **plastic**. The sky was the limit, and so children could saddle not only rocking horses, but also dogs, donkeys, or roosters.

The 21st century, too, favors diverse materials and once again is coming back around to rocking horses, both at home and on the playground. Who wouldn't want to rock around on these spring-loaded animal toys?

I want a carousel and I want a swing

That's how it started.

Gungstol

Rocking chairs

In the beginning, there was a regular chair with curved boards attached to it—rockers which made the chair rock. This happened in the early 18th century, probably in **Great Britain**. Customers found the rocking soothing, and senior citizens relaxed better when sitting in it, rather than in a chair that stayed put. One of the first rocking chairs originated in Sweden. It was called **Gungstol** and it had six legs and would swing pretty widely. Later, famous designers of furniture competed with one another to create the most perfect, beautiful chair. Since people love to be rocked, such chairs are still mass-produced to this day.

Hammocks

Hammocks originated in **South America**, and were likely created by one of its ancient civilizations, such as the Incas, Mayas, or Aztecs. Indigenous Americans used to sleep in beds that were suspended from trees in order to stay protected from dangerous animals at night. When **Christopher Columbus** reached America in the 15th century, hammocks were among the things he discovered there. He took a liking to them, and brought them back to Europe. Originally, suspended beds were used mainly by sailors, but later spread into households. Now, they're pretty standard equipment in any garden.

Carousel

Swinging is not the only movement that's fun; the same goes for spinning, too. But did you know that carousels were originally used by Turkish fighters as **simulators and practice grounds**? While spinning in a circle, the soldiers, using a special pole, tried to knock the hat off a volunteer standing nearby. French nobles, meanwhile, competed to see who would be the first to throw a spear and hit a small ring while riding a carousel. They'd sit on carved horses or in war chariots, spin around, and either win or lose. The first carousels made with fun in mind appeared in 18th-century Europe. They were big, small, or tiny, depending on whether they were fueled by people, mules, or horses.

Seesaws

It's actually **a pretty simple invention**—a propped-up long board with seats at each end so that two children can sit opposite one another and seesaw with no care in the world. The lighter kid spends more time in the air. No one knows who invented this child's ride or where. One way or another, the first written records of children engaging in this type of play come from 1704.

a seesaw

a swing

Swing

Pictures from ancient times clearly show that people have loved swinging from the very beginning. Yes, a simple swing—a seat and two ropes hung from a pole—was invented deep in Antiquity, namely in **Crete** (1450–1300 BC). Later, around the 5th century BC, it spread to Ancient Greece. It was Greece, in fact, where women and children developed a taste for swinging. As centuries went by, swings looked pretty much the same, only the material changed slightly. After the 19th century, manufacturers started paying more attention to the safety aspect of swinging.

TOILETS

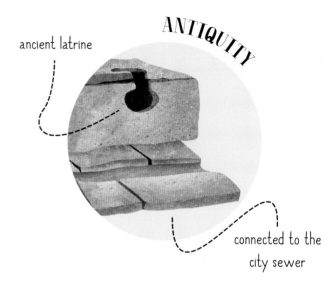

ancient latrine

connected to the city sewer

Uh-oh! When your toilet stops flushing, it's a pretty big deal. What should you do about it? If your dad is handy, he'll have to roll up his sleeves and reach deep inside the toilet to solve the problem. Or would it be better to call a plumber, instead? But what did people do about their poo in the past, anyway?

Civilized antiquity

Ancient Hindus used **water toilets**—a simple board where they could sit comfortably. A drain was below, with water flowing in it to carry all the human waste away. Meanwhile, Egyptians relieved themselves in latrines and used buckets of water to flush. Romans used public latrines, equipped with comfortable seats. While they relieved themselves, they had debates with one another or made important deals. Well, people do get a lot of good ideas in the bathroom, don't they?

In the Colosseum's restroom, there were precisely 25 spots with marble seats and hand-carved armrests. Would you like to relieve yourselves, gentlemen?

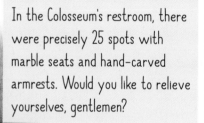

TIMELINE →

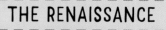

| ANTIQUITY | THE MIDDLE AGES | THE RENAISSANCE |

The Middle Ages

Help, a poo's just landed on me! This could really happen to people who lived in medieval times. That's because the Middle Ages weren't exactly big on hygiene. People would relieve themselves anywhere in the **street** or in the **room**. If you weren't careful walking down a narrow lane, someone might dump their chamber pot on you!

detail of a privy

Through this hole everything fell out.

That's how it worked in the Middle Ages.

privy—exterior and interior

Privy

Castles used to have an **isolated nook** built in a remote corner, with a tiny seat and a hole that opened directly into the moat. You'd just sit down and let it go. Let's spare a moment's thought for the unfortunate passerby below, at the wrong place at the wrong time. And to make the . . . ahem . . . bathroom experience more fun for the noble, live music would often accompany their efforts.

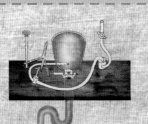

We want comfort!

That's what the nobles thought as centuries passed. After all, nobody likes sitting on a cold rock. Wouldn't it be better to have **an armchair with a built-in pot**? Of course it would! Let's say yes to innovation.

armchair and potty in one

THE RENAISSANCE

Leonardo da Vinci

What is the name of this Renaissance genius doing in a chapter on toilets? Is this some mistake? Not at all! In fact, Leonardo came up with the very first flush toilet. He invented it for one of Francis I of France's castles. It included drainage and ventilation shafts. Unfortunately, this was one of those ideas that was never put into practice.

Don't you forget that!

The name is **Sir John Harrington**, a relative of the British Queen Victoria. The calendar shows it's the end of the 16th century. And what does Harrington do? He invents the **flush toilet**—two models, while he's at it. Sadly, none of them or the original designs have survived to this day, so we have no choice but to believe this really happened . . .

Sir John Harrington

TIMELINE ⟶

ANTIQUITY	THE MIDDLE AGES	THE RENAISSANCE

Unless there were other options the corner of the hall was sufficient.

The stool of the Louises

The children of Louis XIV—the so-called **Sun King**—loved their special defecation stool with a hole in it. Louis XV himself regularly held audiences while sitting on it. His son, Louis XVI, employed two noble servants who were the only ones allowed to take the stool out. These noble servants were conferred the title of "Knight of the toilet paper." Enviable, isn't it?

17TH–18TH CENTURY

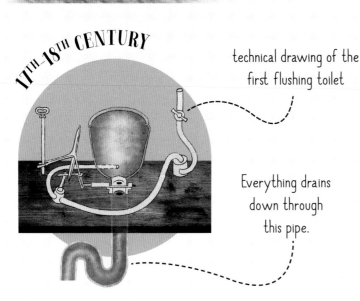

technical drawing of the first flushing toilet

Everything drains down through this pipe.

Alexander Cumming

The era of flushing

Who can we thank for this? **Alexander Cumming**, who decided at the end of the 18th century to invent a real toilet, with a trap, flusher, and water seal. But few people could afford something so unusual and high-class. Regular citizens had to stick with their potties and defecation stools.

18TH CENTURY	19TH CENTURY	20TH CENTURY

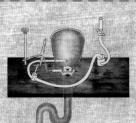

The 19th century

This era brought luxurious bowls and potties built in even more luxurious chests and armchairs, until it ended up with porcelain toilets, drain pipes, and flushers. Before long, the flush toilet conquered the world.

Built-in potties lasted till the end of the 19th century.

portable, space-saving, and handy

sneak peek into the outhouse

Good old outhouses

Although we've been flushing since the 19th century as if our lives depend on it, we don't say no to a regular old, uncomfortable **outhouse** when the going gets tough. The outhouse has lived to see many centuries, and will survive many more. And if there's no way around it, we still relieve ourselves out in the open, hidden behind a tree—just like our prehistoric great-grandfathers and grandmothers used to do. Scientists theorize that this way of relieving ourselves is the most natural and healthy for our bodies.

20TH CENTURY

one of the most expensive toilets in the world

material 18-karat gold

Yippee! Ever since the 20th century, we've been able to truly enjoy our time in the bathroom—you can sit there, think, read poetry, or browse through newspapers and magazines if you're more practically minded. Everything ugly and unnecessary is then flushed down—*shhhhhh*—and it's gone. Dreamers may spend their time in the room wondering what it would be like to pee and poop into a bowl made from gold. No, that's not fiction—one such toilet really does exist. You can admire it in New York's Guggenheim Museum, and not only that—you can actually relieve yourself in this 18-karat piece. In New York, anything goes.

TIMELINE ⟶

| ANTIQUITY | THE MIDDLE AGES | THE RENAISSANCE |

Ecological super-toilet

Friendliness is a trend in our modern times. We're power-friendly, water-friendly, and we try to be as **environmentally friendly** as possible. That's where the good old toilet issue arises—can you be water-friendly while flushing? *Whee!* tumbles the precious waterfall down the sewers, and Mother Earth cries for help. But people fortunately always figure out what to do sooner or later, and have come up with a super-hyper-ultra-modern toilet with a washer, all in one—a special system that takes the water you use to wash your hands, and uses it to flush anything that needs to be flushed.

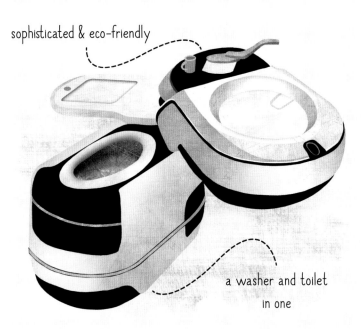

sophisticated & eco-friendly

a washer and toilet in one

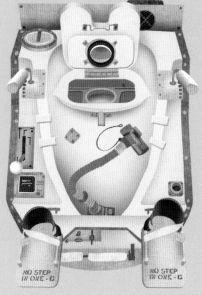

The need to relieve oneself doesn't go away just because you're an astronaut in outer space. But zero gravity makes things a *wee* bit complicated, so to speak. That's why bathrooms in space stations have foot holders and anatomically shaped seats.

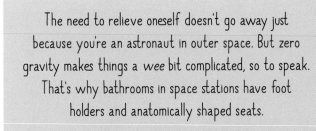

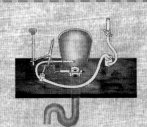

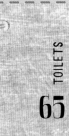

Paper, tissue, mirrors, and bathtubs

paper tissues

a public fountain

Handkerchiefs

A long time ago, it was a sign of dignity and nobility to carry a handkerchief. Ancient Greeks adorned their clothes with it and used it only for wiping their sweaty foreheads. As centuries passed, France experimented with the size and shape of handkerchiefs and viewed them as important fashion accessories. There were tiny ones, or inwrought ones, as large as headscarves. These ones were very valuable. No wonder commoners were **downright forbidden** from carrying handkerchiefs in the 16th century. On the other hand, the 20th century allowed people to blow their noses into them, and came up with disposable paper tissues to boot.

Washbasins and bathtubs

Lying in the bathtub and lounging around—fantastic, right? But could our great-great-grand ancestors afford such luxury? No, they had to do with a bucket of water or **a public fountain**. The craftier ones would soak themselves in **a barrel** made of wooden slats. It was recommended to line the tub with a piece of canvas so that you wouldn't get a splinter. Hands were washed in **a lavabo**—a copper, tin, or iron washbasin with a pitcher. And where was the first ceramic washbasin built? In Ancient Asia. With the exception of Ancient Greece, Europe had to wait a few centuries longer for it.

a barrel

a comfortable bathtub

a wall-mounted washbasin

a lavabo

Venetian mirror

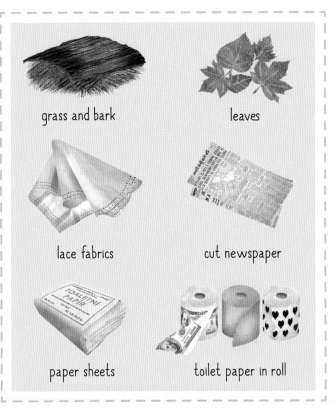

grass and bark

leaves

lace fabrics

cut newspaper

paper sheets

toilet paper in roll

Toilet paper

If you believe that toilet paper has always been a part of toilets, you're wrong. In the past, to clean yourself, you had to make do with some **straw**, **hay**, or **moss**. The rich had pieces of soft fabric or lace at their disposal. In some countries, people wiped their butts with water and their hand—yikes! Finally, the 19th century came up with **books of thin silky paper**. Meanwhile in China, the locals have pampered their butts with **toilet paper** since Antiquity. Impressively, the first records of this are from the 6th century AD. How come? Well, China did invent paper, so they were mostly already there.

Ancient Egyptian

Gothic

Renaissance

Baroque

Mirrors

It's an integral part of the world of hygiene. Originally, your **reflection on the water's surface** was enough to check your face. In the long-ago 6th century BC, our image-conscious ancestors learned how to polish **slabs of obsidian**, thereby making the very first mirrors. Four centuries later—in the Bronze Age—the volcanic glass (obsidian) was replaced with **polished bronze** and **silver**. The original glass mirrors were made in medieval Venice. Back then, craftsmen applied a mixture of mercury and tin to the back of the glass, and voilà—the reflection was almost perfect.

a reflection on the water's surface

TOOTHBRUSHES

Raise your hands—who enjoys brushing their teeth? And now, those of you who don't like to brush your teeth and whose mom has to force you to do it, raise your hands. There's more of the latter, despite the fact that dental hygiene is incredibly important. Anyway, when did people first realize that they couldn't do without it before going to sleep or after getting up to greet the new day? Who came up with the tools and when? Was it a long time ago? Or recently?

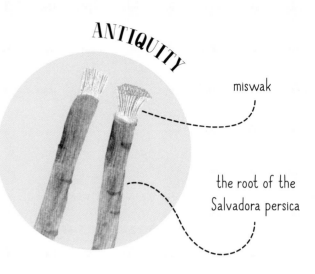

ANTIQUITY

miswak

the root of the Salvadora persica

The things that the Egyptian dead packed for the afterlife also attest to the importance of dental hygiene. Chewing sticks were definitely included!

1,800 BCE

The story of the toothbrush goes somewhat like this: We're in ancient **Mesopotamia**, around the year 1,800 BCE. In order to drive a hurtful pest—cavities—out of their mouths, people bite down on sticks. Ancient Egyptians, Greeks, and Romans brushed their teeth in the same way. They'd chew on the stick and gnaw at it for so long that it frayed at one end, remotely resembling . . . well, what do you think? A toothbrush, of course!

15th century AD

As Christopher Columbus reached America, **the Chinese** made the very first actual toothbrush—with bristles! Did such toothbrushes have any drawbacks? They did—the bristles were too hard and rough. Nothing that would get Europeans going, let me tell you that. At least when merchants and seafarers brought Chinese toothbrushes to Europe, European customers didn't exactly bend over backwards to get them.

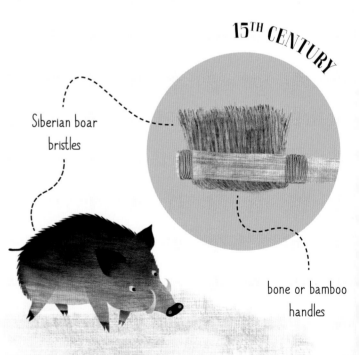

15TH CENTURY

Siberian boar bristles

bone or bamboo handles

TIMELINE →

ANTIQUITY

15TH CENTURY

A bit of boredom

A bit of boredom can be good for you, sometimes . . . That's because you can get some really great ideas when you're bored. **William Addis** surely did. When he was in prison, he made his own toothbrush by sticking broom bristles into a bone left over from his meal, and that was it! When did this happen? In 1780! Busy hands are happy hands. Once he was free, the toothbrush made him, and later his son, very rich.

William Addis 1780

Before the modern toothbrush arrived, there was the common broom.

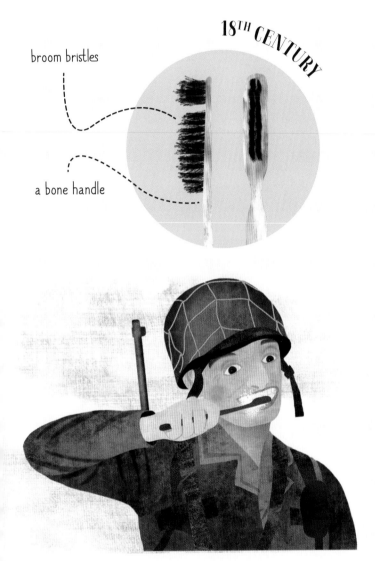

18ᵀᴴ CENTURY

broom bristles

a bone handle

Like a soldier

Military discipline included **strict dental hygiene**. During WWII, American soldiers had to brush their teeth regularly, every morning and night, in order to keep them healthy. Can you imagine what it would be like to fight while your teeth are aching?

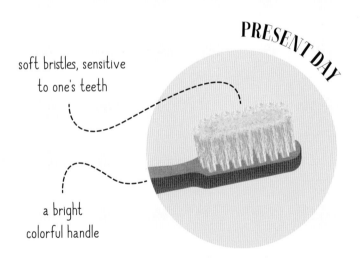

PRESENT DAY

soft bristles, sensitive to one's teeth

a bright colorful handle

The 20th century introduced **plastic** and **nylon**. A veritable flood of toothbrushes followed, each one a different color, size, and shape. Even electric toothbrushes!

18ᵀᴴ CENTURY

PRESENT DAY

Straightening and brushing your teeth

modern invisible braces

Brace it with braces

Nice straight teeth were desired as early as the Etruscan civilization around the 6th century BCE. And so Etruscans came up with a tool that would make their teeth straighter—**braces**. How do we know this? Due to archeological excavations. If an Etruscan's tooth became loose, they'd simply bind it with a golden wire. In the Middle Ages, gold and silver were the foundation of almost all braces. But the science of straightening teeth—orthodontics—wasn't properly established until the 18th century.

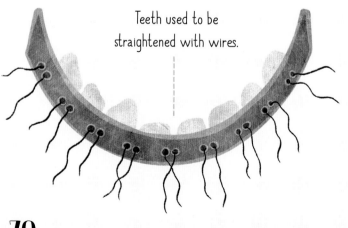

Teeth used to be straightened with wires.

Not without my toothpick!

Having pieces of food stuck between your teeth was pretty uncomfortable even back then. And so Mr. Homo Sapiens found a piece of wood or bone, excused himself, and eliminated the problem. Under the reign of Louis XIV—the Sun King—toothpicks were a luxury item, made from **gold** and decorated with more gemstones. When attending a feast, the noble guests had their own toothpicks. The year? 1860. The place? America. **Charles Foster** has just started mass-producing ordinary toothpicks.

an aristocrat from the Louis XIV era

Dental replacement

We already know that Etruscans were suckers for nice teeth. But also, if their teeth were found lacking, they would take **an animal tooth**, sink it into a golden holder, and attach it to their gum. Other nations molded fake teeth from ivory and fixed them with golden wires. And those unfortunate enough to be enslaved and cursed with beautiful teeth were sometimes forced to give a tooth or two to their dentally impaired master. At the end of the 18th century, **Nicolas Dubois de Chermant** invented porcelain dentures.

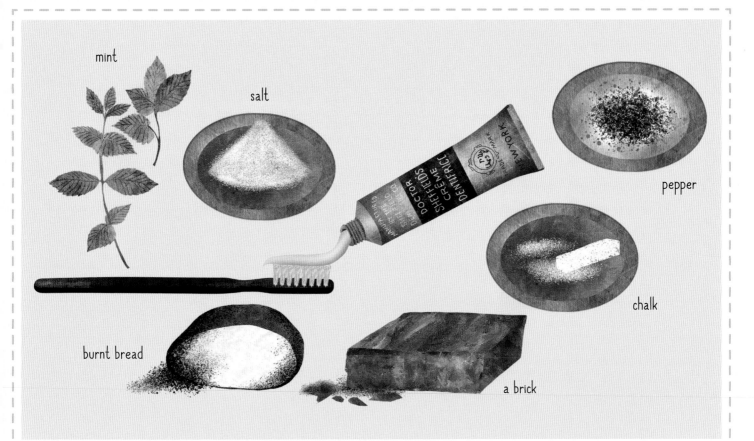

mint

salt

pepper

chalk

burnt bread

a brick

Toothpaste

Salt, mint, a bit of pepper, and other spices. Those were the first mixtures that helped people brush their teeth thoroughly and have pleasant breath. When and where? In Ancient Egypt and China. Well, different countries have different customs. If you lived in the 18th century, you'd brush your teeth with a powder made from burnt bread. A few centuries later, you'd do with ground bricks, mixed with salt and chalk. In **1850**, the very first creamy toothpaste appeared on the market. Originally, it was sold in **jars**.

an enslaved man with beautiful teeth

dentures

BEDS

No child likes going to bed at night. Their parents chase them around without compromise, regardless of whether the tots are right in the middle of an incredibly adventurous game, or not. Meanwhile, grandmas and grandpas love to lay their weary bones down on soft mattresses. Judging from this, was it some old man or woman who invented beds? Or does the story go somewhat differently?

Dry leaves and grass

At the beginning, there was a pile of **dry leaves and grass**, maybe some moss. Our prehistoric ancestors would happily nestle down in such a bed, and enjoy sweet dreams of juicy mammoth roasts or necklaces made from river pebbles.

grass in place of a mattress

PREHISTORY

More grass makes for softer sleeping.

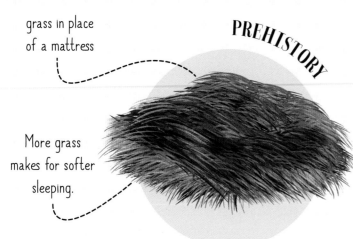

Nothing like warm skin

Later, a couple of whiners piped up that leaves weren't enough, so they covered themselves with **the skin** of an animal the pack had hunted. The hairier the pelt, the warmer and more comfortable it was for the sleeper. And there was one other advantage! The pelt could be moved from one place to another. All one needed to do was roll it up, shove it under their arm, and off they went. This simply wasn't possible with dry leaves.

One day, someone took two pieces of animal pelt, sewed them together, and stuffed the bag full—with leaves, grass, and moss, of course. Guess what they ended up with? An actual bed—comfortable, soft, one on which the sleeper could sprawl out. No one needed to be forced to lie in such a bed—on the contrary! There's nothing better than sweet dreams.

TIMELINE ⟶

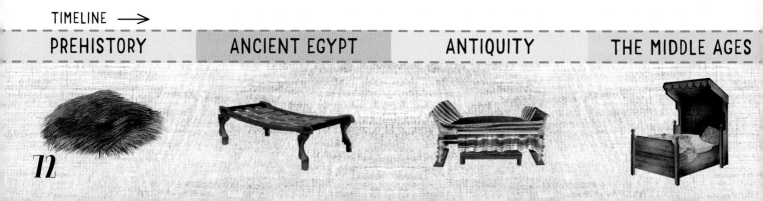

PREHISTORY   ANCIENT EGYPT   ANTIQUITY   THE MIDDLE AGES

12

How well did Egyptians sleep?

Only high-ranking members of Egyptian society could afford a real bed with **a wooden frame** and **mats** woven from straw. The less wealthy had to do with a regular mat placed on the floor, or a hard bench made from unfired bricks and shoved to the wall. On the other hand, pharaohs never went anywhere without having their own folding beds at hand.

luxurious bedding of pharaohs

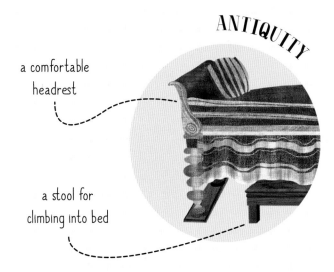

ANCIENT EGYPT

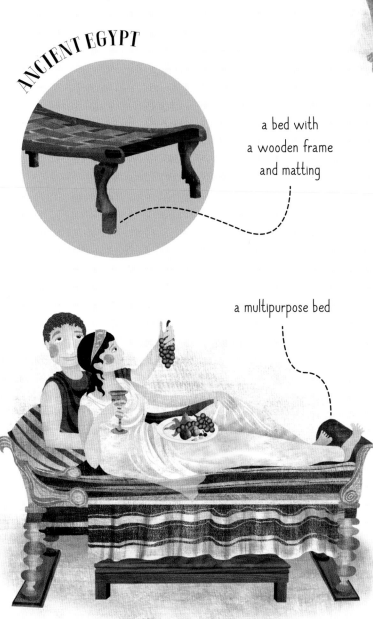

a bed with a wooden frame and matting

The first double bed

The first ever double bed was made in Ancient Rome. The majestic piece of furniture took up almost an entire bedroom and was so tall its owners had **to climb a stool** in order to get in. Ancient beds weren't for sleeping only, though. There were special types of couches where one could eat, drink, chat, or work.

a multipurpose bed

ANTIQUITY

a comfortable headrest

a stool for climbing into bed

THE RENAISSANCE   THE BAROQUE   THE REGENCY ERA   19TH–20TH CENTURY

The Middle Ages

In the early Middle Ages, light ancient beds were replaced with ones that were shaped like **a chest**. You crawled in, covered yourself, and were good to go. Later, the chest was raised higher above the floor and supplemented with drawers that could fit another sleeper—now that's what we call sleeping in style! Yes, medieval beds really could accommodate an entire family—and its servant.

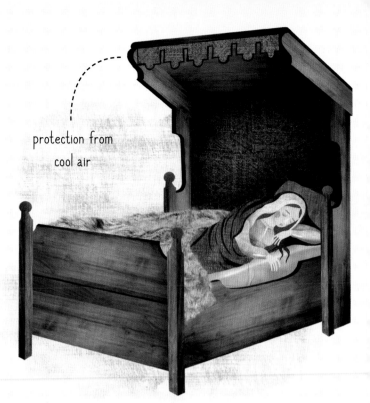

protection from cool air

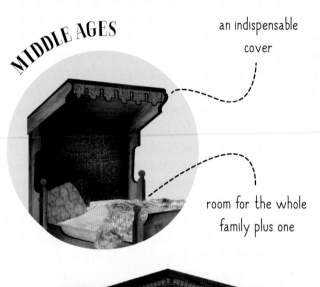

MIDDLE AGES

an indispensable cover

room for the whole family plus one

It's drafty in here

Drafty, you say? Don't worry. We'll place **a small wooden roof** above the bed, and we're all set. Yes, that's how those who loved long nights of uninterrupted sleep used to think in the Middle Ages. Later, the wooden roof was enhanced with **pleated drapes** to make sure the sleeper could enjoy their privacy. And canopies had another benefit: no mosquitos would get in, or heat out.

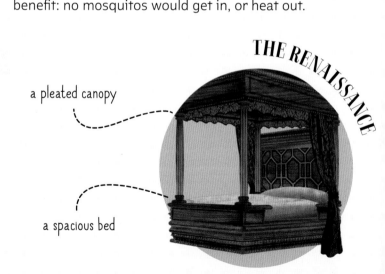

THE RENAISSANCE

a pleated canopy

a spacious bed

TIMELINE ⟶

| PREHISTORY | ANCIENT EGYPT | ANTIQUITY | THE MIDDLE AGES |

The Baroque period

In Baroque times, beds were where the action was. Rich feudal lords and their wives received important visitors and made important decisions **while lying down**. And why wouldn't they? Comfort above all else! Long live comfort! Back then, lying was considered the noblest position one could assume.

THE BAROQUE

a noble in the most noble position

royal sleeping

Sailing into the 19th century

The Regency period—an **era of a strict, stark, military style**. The tastes which prevailed at this time also dictated how sleeping looked—no luxury arrangements, but rather simple beds shaped like a chest, with pleated curtains hung from a soft canopy. There's a reason why this type of furniture resembled a ship—it was a symbol of our voyage down the river of life.

to lie down and enter the realm of dreams

REGENCY STYLE

fine ornaments

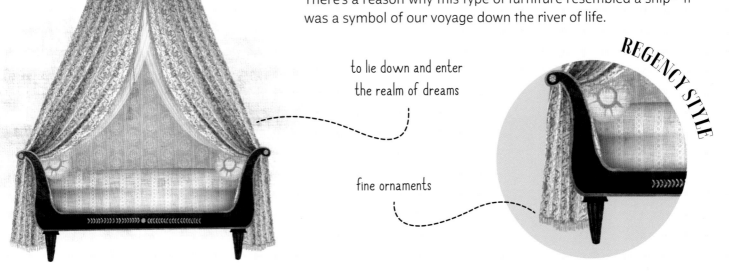

THE RENAISSANCE	THE BAROQUE	THE REGENCY ERA	19ᵀᴴ–20ᵀᴴ CENTURY

Be careful, we tilt!

For years, beds maintained their simple shape. Over time, wood was replaced with metal, sometimes with upholstery. Later, ornaments took a backseat as new preferences emerged and people became more interested in the bed being comfortable and safe. The Romantic era invented **the easy-to-store tilt bed**, while the 20th century introduced special adjustable beds.

a tilt bed

19ᵀᴴ–20ᵀᴴ CENTURY

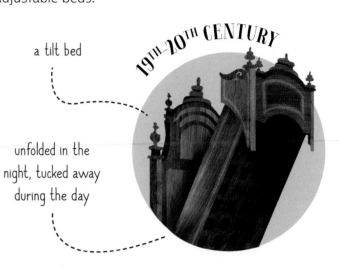

unfolded in the night, tucked away during the day

Mom, come down the slide!

Every child dreams of being able to play all the time, not go to bed, and not get up too early in the morning. And if they have a super-duper playbed with a slide, that's a whole other level of fun. During the day, you can rollick in your bedroom as if it were a playground. And in the morning? The slide does wonders—rub the sleep from your eyes, sit up, and wee! You're on the floor. Prehistoric children who slept on regular grass would have turned green with envy.

A slide is great fun for both parents and their children.

Who will sleep up top?

The ladder can also be used for stretching.

TIMELINE ⟶

| PREHISTORY | ANCIENT EGYPT | ANTIQUITY | THE MIDDLE AGES |

the practical 20th century ------

storage space -----

Three in one

Uh-oh, what to do if your bedroom is ridiculously tiny? Where will the children sleep? Where will their toys fit? The practical 20th century found the answer. What about a bed with **additional storage space**? The younger sibling can do with the extended mattress and the plush toys will enjoy their stay in the drawer.

a couch during the day

Space for a bed?

If you have a tiny apartment that can't fit a bed, there's no need to feel sad. Just get a sofa bed. You can rest on it during the day, and once night falls, take the mattress out—bam! The sofa turns into a comfortable bed, as if by magic. The time of origin? The 20th century, of course.

A couch? Or a bed?

a bed during the night

It wouldn't be the 20th century if this ingenious, **budget-friendly invention** wasn't further perfected. Simply put, the sofa's sitting part is separated from the mattress, which is placed at the bottom of the sofa and used only for sleeping.

THE RENAISSANCE	THE BAROQUE	THE REGENCY ERA	19TH–20TH CENTURY

BEDS

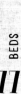

17

Everything from beds to carpets

She doesn't like the sun!

The carpet boom

The carpet industry kicked off in the 16th century in **India and Persia**. Carpets just look so good in opulent palaces! Until the 19th century, only the wealthy classes could afford them, both in Asia and in Europe. Common people couldn't afford to splurge on such a luxury item. So what did they use to make their floors more comfortable? Reed, for example.

Blinds

Originally, they were nothing but bars in windows, like those found in Asian palaces. But of course, they couldn't be rolled up. The progressive 18th century, however, introduced the very first blinds—ordinary shades that couldn't be adjusted, but were still a bit better than bars. The even more progressive 19th century came up with the **adjustable blades** we know today. Or rather, a French joiner named Cochot did. He had the blinds patented, and the world went crazy for them.

The Trojan War is over. The victorious Agamemnon, the king of Mycenae, is finally coming home. But uh-oh! His wife has already found a replacement—his cousin Aigisthos. What a pickle! So, the lovers rolled out a carpet, which led the war hero all the way to the feast hall. But once there, he found no delicious roast. Instead . . . the couple had him murdered. But the red blood of the deceived soaked into the ceremonial carpet and has been reminding us of this murder to this day.

Agamemnon, the King of Mycenae

the insidious Aigisthos

the unfaithful woman

Carpets

Imagine the cold and hostile climate of the Central Asian steppes. Members of **nomadic tribes** are huddling in their tents. What do they do to feel better? They weave carpets that will be placed on the ground in order to thermally insulate it, but also on the walls of their homes to make them look nicer. It's so simple. A weaving loom consists of wooden frames, with warp threads mounted on them. What time is this, again? A long time ago—about 400 BCE.

Curtains

Yes, curtains were also born from that first Neolithic skin flapping in **the cave entrance**. In short, they weren't that different from drapes, up until the 15th century, when housewives started hanging light crocheted or silk textiles next to their heavy drapes. And that was it. At the same time, the first lace began to be made so it's obvious which turn curtains took next.

TIGHTS

When it's cold and snowy outside, children wear tights under their trousers. "It's so that you're warm and don't catch cold," moms say to their protesting tots. But no one's really into them. Boys are kind of ashamed of their tights. What about girls? They frown, wanting to have a few choice words with the genius who came up with these stupid things. Who was he, anyway, and how did those darned tights come to be?

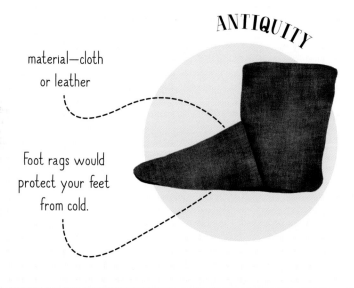

Even Roman soldiers protected their legs with cloth.

Greek foot rugs

Antiquity

Even Ancient Egyptians wore **woolen tights**. We learned this when a couple of tombs, built in the 3rd–6th century AD, gave up their secrets. Meanwhile, Ancient Greeks loved to wrap their legs in long strips of fabric or leather, stitched together. It wasn't about finery. Instead, these strange tights had one clear purpose—**to protect one's legs**.

ANTIQUITY

material—cloth or leather

Foot rags would protect your feet from cold.

TIMELINE →

| ANTIQUITY | THE MIDDLE AGES | THE RENAISSANCE |

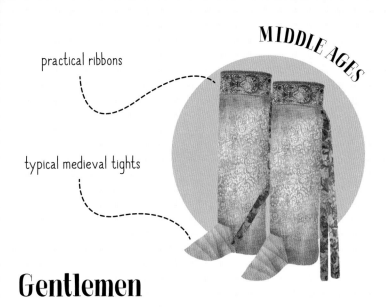

practical ribbons

typical medieval tights

Gentlemen

In the 12th century, **European men**—yes, you've read that correctly, this applied to gentlemen only—took great pleasure in wearing tights. And why wouldn't they? Tights were in, back then. Medieval whippersnappers and fops wouldn't go outside in anything that wasn't a pair of tight trousers that reached all the way from the waist to their feet. The trousers looked like leggings do today, and guys were pretty proud of them. The more courageous among them wore pairs with each leg a different color.

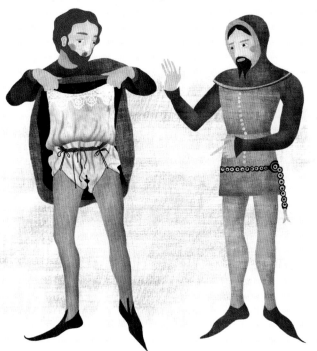

Ladies

Medieval ladies also got their money's worth. Though it's as clear as day that unlike men, women had to hide their tights under a skirt. So it was all right if women's tights reached only just below the knees, where they would be tied with ribbons. And what kind of material went into men's and women's tights? Leather or ordinary fabric.

| 17TH–18TH CENTURY | 19TH CENTURY | 20TH–21ST CENTURY |

TIGHTS

Aesthetics above all

In the mid-16th century, Renaissance fashion-istas improved their wardrobes with some choice pairs of tights—silk, hand-knitted, and incredibly expensive. Their practical purpose gave way to **aesthetics**. The poor and commoners had no choice but to stare in silent admiration and secret envy at how the rich guys once again squandered a fortune for a piece of finery.

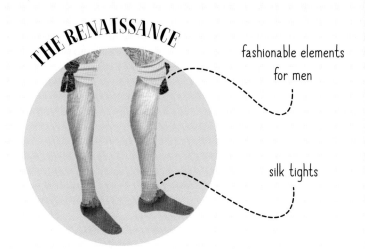

THE RENAISSANCE

fashionable elements for men

silk tights

I knit, you knit, we knit

Phew! It's 1589 and the very first mechanical knitting machine has finally been invented. A crafty English priest named **William Lee** came up with it, bringing about a real tight revolution. That's because fashion accessories that were made by using modern methods—with machines—were much softer and luxurious than their hand-knitted counterparts. At any rate, the high prices remained despite the speedy production. Why? Because of the luxury materials. Silk isn't free, you know?

William Lee

1562

1590

1620

Fashion fads of the Renaissance

1640

TIMELINE →

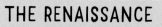

ANTIQUITY   THE MIDDLE AGES   THE RENAISSANCE

The more tights, the better

Especially if it's **cold outside**. Noble fans of tights treated themselves to several layers of the silky finery. One pair, another one on top of it, and then the third one to crown it all. Why not? After all, the aristocrats could more than afford it.

typical tights with lace hemming

not even high boots could do away with tights

a typical 17th-century chevalier

a detail of a folded-down lacy hem

Where to put your tights?

We have another fad over here: **high leather boots**, for special occasions and bad weather. Well, that's nice, but what should the 17th-century fashionistas do if they don't want to give up their tights—or God forbid, tear them apart in those fancy shoes? The solution was simple: the fops wore yet another pair over the soft silk, made from somewhat coarser fabric, and folded the lacy hem over the edge of their boots. Now, that looked great!

Chevaliers in tights

Throughout the 17th and 18th centuries, tights were an integral, indispensable part of men's wardrobe. They were made from silk and stayed in place due to special garters. If it was freezing outside, a single silk layer definitely wouldn't keep the wearer warm, which is why the fops put one layer on their thin legs after another. One pair of tights, then another, and a third one on top of that—why not? Anything not to be cold—if they could afford it, that is. The poor were simply out of luck and had to stay chilly.

17TH–18TH CENTURY	19TH CENTURY	20TH–21ST CENTURY

Tights? Too feminine!

Turning up his nose at this piece of underwear, the early 19th-century man preferred to put on socks. While the entire 18th century was essentially the era of men's tights—or leggings—new fashion trends brought about trousers as we know them, and **men stopped enjoying tights**. Meanwhile, ladies switched to the first seamless stockings. But a small mistake had crept in: the novelty couldn't stay up on the leg, so girls and women had to constantly pull their stockings up.

19TH CENTURY

patterned tights to be worn under a long skirt

a typical 19th-century girl

Tights needed to be put on carefully.

One disadvantage to tights—they wouldn't stay up.

Ah, real nylons

The year's 1940, and America's celebrating the invention of **a new artificial fiber**—nylon. All girls are rejoicing and prettying themselves up. Nylon stockings—or *nylons*, for short—are pretty affordable, but unavailable for purchase. Don't throw your hands up, though—just draw a straight seam on your bare leg, and nobody will know that you have nothing on. Nylon tights and stockings ultimately beat the silk version in the 1960s. Long live the nylon, all hail the fallen silk!

Goodbye to silk stockings!

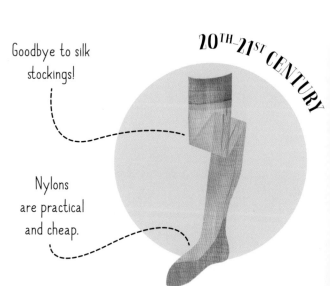

20TH–21ST CENTURY

Nylons are practical and cheap.

TIMELINE →

| ANTIQUITY | THE MIDDLE AGES | THE RENAISSANCE |

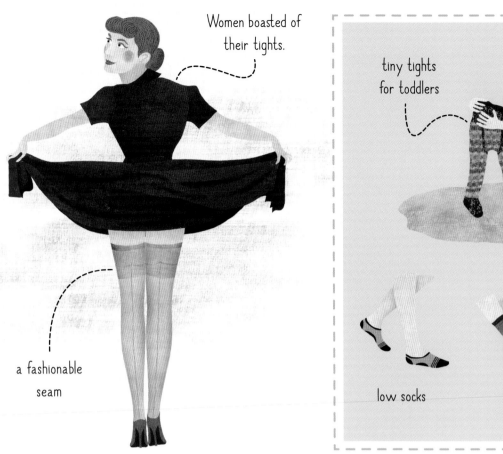

Women boasted of their tights.

a fashionable seam

tiny tights for toddlers

But the mom needs to help with dressing.

low socks

toe socks

sports socks

Stockings of all kinds

Tights for toddlers, children, young ladies, and adult women. Colorful, funny, and neutral, tights to be worn at home, in kindergarten, underneath trousers, and with miniskirts. Our modern times certainly **aren't short on ideas**. Harsh winters warrant insulated thermo-tights, which make sure your knees won't freeze or just get cold. Our ancestors, dressed in layers upon layers of silk tights, would stare in astonishment at such a convenience. And if a girl wants to look her best, she doesn't have to limit herself to a regular old seam, the hit of the mid-20th century! Modern women can show off their legs in tights that have dots, patches, checkers, mesh, even snake-skin patterns. The possibilities are infinite.

17TH–18TH CENTURY

19TH CENTURY

20TH–21ST CENTURY

TIGHTS

Accessories to spice up your style

two-toed socks fitted for Egyptian sandals

Bow ties

The bow tie, too, flew all the way from Croatia, on the wings of the scarves worn by Croatian hussars. It was just another way of tying a scarf around your neck. Once again, bow ties were all the rage with the French, who loved fashion, so they conquered the male necks of the 17th and 18th centuries. It's the 19th century. **Beau Brummel**, an English dandy, just loves beautiful clothing. It was he who made men's suits a success.

Beau Brummel
1735–1803

Socks

At the beginning of everything, there were the prehistoric times, and with them, some pretty **cold feet**. An inventive ancestor of ours—maybe the one who was the most sensitive to the cold—got angry one day and simply wrapped his chilly feet in a piece of animal pelt. Let there be warmth! The oldest surviving pair of woolen socks was found in Egypt. The date of their making? The 3rd-5th century. They had only two toes so that they could be comfortably worn in sandals. Ancient Greeks made their feet feel warmer with the so-called **piloi**—socks weaved out of animal hairs. Meanwhile, Romans used to wear **udones**—socks made from pieces of fabric, felt, or leather. The drawback? Little to no flexibility. Simply put, they would constantly fall off your feet.

Bow ties untied and tied

Ties

It's the 17th century, and the Thirty Years' War is raging. Young Croatian men are being called to arms. Their girlfriends are crying. Each one's giving her boyfriend the scarf she usually wears around her shoulders. The young soldiers tie the scarves around their necks. Meanwhile, officers receive somewhat finer shawls—lacy, silky, fluffy. They look good, too. It was these scarves that caught the attention of French fashionistas, who used to suffocate in their stiffened collars. So they set them aside and started wearing scarves, tied in the Croatian style—**á la Croate**.

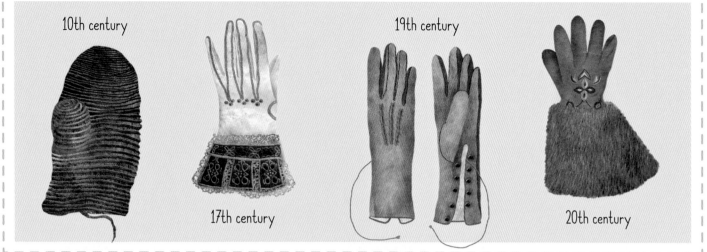

10th century

17th century

19th century

20th century

What about hands

Even our ancestors, the prehistoric hunters, used to wear **fur mittens** that protected them from the harsh elements. Living in the Ice Age was no picnic, you know. Later, in Ancient Egypt, women used special small pockets without holes to protect the beauty of their hands. Even pharaohs wore them—as a symbol of their high position. Over the centuries, long gloves have become an essential part of every woman's wardrobe. Noble ladies boasted gloves that were embroidered and decorated with precious stones! It wasn't until the late 20th century that gloves had a comeback as **a practical accessory**.

Foot rags would protect your feet from the cold.

high leather boots

Footwraps, or socks, for both a cornfield and a battlefield

Why are you so surprised? It's soldiers and practical farmers who are to blame for socks, after all. One day, they took a piece of fabric, wrapped it around the bottom part of their foot, tied it with a string, and voilà! They had a beautiful **footwrap**. As soon as it got dirty, the wearer washed it, dried it, and the "sock" was once again as good as new.

ENCYCLOPEDIA OF ORDINARY THINGS

© B4U Publishing for Albatros,
an imprint of Albatros Media Group, 2021
5. května 1746/22, Prague 4, Czech Republic
Printed in China by Leo Paper Group
Written by Štěpánka Sekaninová
Illustrated by Eva Chupíková
Translated by Radka Knotková
Edited by Scott Alexander Jones

www.albatrosbooks.com

Until they break down, we often don't realize the importance of the things we have. Take the toilet, for instance—if it doesn't work, it's a disaster! You can find the chapter about what toilets looked like in the past on page 60.

When did the first tights and cozy socks appear? And who invented them?
You'll find out in a chapter about all sorts of tights and socks on page 80.